BORDERING ON THE RIDICULOUS

BORDERING ON THE RIDICULOUS

JON COOK

First published in Great Britain in 2022 by
Bannister Publications Ltd
118 Saltergate, Chesterfield, Derbyshire S40 1NG

ISBN: 978-1-909813-87-8

Typeset by Bannister Publications Ltd

Printed and bound in Great Britain

This book was self-published by Bannister Publications.
For more information on self-publishing visit:
www.bannisterpublications.com

CONTENTS

Foreword vii
Introduction xi

1. Ministry of Barriers, Walls and Fences 1
2. Arbitrary and Absurd Borders 39
3. Cool Border Crossings / Running across Borders 51
4. Border Errors / Map Wars / Mysteries 76
5. To be an Enclave or an Exclave 91
6. Quirky Borders 114
7. Angry or Disputed Borders 134
8. Life without borders in the future 153
   Conclusion 160

Illustrations 167
References 169
Index 173
Acknowledgments 178

FOREWORD

Borders are very much in the news! They define our territorial boundaries of necessity but not, hopefully our minds. Jon Cook, in a thoughtful and entertaining work on the subject, challenges us to think outside the box on the role of borders and our approach to them. I am particularly grateful to him in my role as outgoing Chair of Book Aid International, to whom he has donated a contribution from the proceeds of "Bordering on the Ridiculous".

My own life has been lived on two continents, Africa and Europe, in which I have been privileged to grow up and work as a lawyer, parliamentarian, and diplomat. Borders in Africa are often literally "ridiculous" drawn up by cartographers at the behest of politicians, many of whom had never been there or had any understanding or care for its topography or the cultures of its peoples. They sought in the Treaty of Berlin to carve up a continent between the Great Powers of Europe entirely for their own benefit and with little or no regard to the tribal linguistic and cultural realities on the ground. The resulting conflicts continue to be worked out in modern Africa, as exemplified by events in Sudan, Somaliland, the Sahel, and Cameroon.

The last of these is particularly tragic as it has involved the mass dislocation of more than a million peoples and the slaughter of innocent civilians, all with little or no comment in Britain and France, whose competing languages and legal systems are at the heart of the conflict.

Boundaries in this context between different provinces take on a literal life or death dimension. Book Aid International is providing books in specially designed boxes distributed by our brave local partners to hundreds of thousands of displaced persons hiding in the equatorial bush. Books and the kingdom of the mind provide a place of respite for otherwise beleaguered peoples. We take no side providing books on both sides of the border, just as we do to refugees, on both sides of the Mediterranean.

Borders cease to have any meaning when the written world transcends them to unite peoples in common humanity. "No man is an island, entire of itself; every man is a piece of the continent, a part of the main."

John Donne goes on to write, "If a clod be washed away by the Sea, Europe is the less". I am writing these words in my library in a home that looks over the Channel towards France. I walk along the shoreline and pass by a Station of the National Coastwatch Institution (NCI). Each station is manned by a team of fully trained volunteers who keep a daylight watch around the British Isles. In 57 stations, over 2500 of these dedicated men and women provide a vital link with the Coast Guard and Border Forces protecting our shores. They protect the Borders of "this sceptred isle" and the lives, regardless of rank or origin of those who get into trouble on or by the sea. We should spare a thought for them when we think about what borders mean in practice today as for some people; they mean risking all simply to get over them for others risking much to protect them.

Borders, as Jon Cook so well illustrates, are not fixed but change in time and circumstances of our own have changed with Brexit. We are still working through the consequences of that, not least on the island of Ireland, where faith and the "Border" delineate distinct identities.

Managing identity in the midst of so much change and uncertainty represents one of the greatest challenges of our time. The truth is that despite a borderless World Wide Web and a greater degree of "Connectivity" than at any time in human history, for many there has been an increase in the sense of alienation and separation from "the other" and others. We are all too easily trapped in a world delineated by our own preferences and prejudices fed to us in an endless loop on our mobile devices.

Books and libraries in such a world become all the more important. They permit new insights unsought after and unexpected revelations, and exciting encounters with other worlds and experiences. Often the result of chance encounters when a book cover catches our attention, or a book falls open on a page. I am forever grateful for the broadening of experience that books have given me. There is no more worthwhile activity than sharing the opportunity to access books with others.

Books above anything else defy all Borders! That is why so often those who seek to limit thought and movement too burn them whenever they are allowed to do so. We need to be constantly vigilant in denying them the space or opportunity to do that. The world of the mind is one in which we can roam freely without borders. In reading this book, we can celebrate that fact as we contemplate the nature of borders themselves.

The Rt Hon. the Lord Boateng PC DL

INTRODUCTION

They come to build a wall between us. We know they won't win.

**"DON'T DREAM IT'S OVER" BY
CROWDED HOUSE**

My interest in borders started with an identity crisis – I was born in Widnes, Lancashire and the county border changed when I was 11 so we ended up in Cheshire, without us moving house! For years afterwards, residents would address the envelopes of letters with Widnes, Lancashire instead of the more upmarket Cheshire. I attended school in Merseyside and played rugby for Yorkshire Universities and then represented English Universities and even more confusingly was selected for Great Britain Universities and Colleges. I am still waiting for a call-up for the United Kingdom athletics team!

The natural border for Lancashire and Cheshire was well defined as the river Mersey, but when I was living in Widnes there was nothing clear about the waters of the Mersey! Its banks were littered with the industry of the north-west, such as *Fisons* fertiliser factory in Widnes and the chemical giant at the time, *ICI* in Runcorn, polluting this natural fluvial border almost at will. Perhaps my obsession with borders started here at the location of the narrow bridging point along the river Mersey.

The name Mersey originates from the Queen of Mercia, who was called Queen Ethelfleda, and is the Saxon word for border or boundary people. In the seventh century this river became the border between Northumbria and Mercia. There are not many people who know that one of the three bridges here, the rail viaduct built in 1868 from Widnes to Runcorn, is called Ethelfleda bridge. Indeed, there is evidence that her burh (pronounced burx) or fortification built in 915 was at the location of one of the viaduct towers. Some locals suggest that the towers were castellated as a reminder of this former stronghold. If you ever venture into Runcorn, outside the Brindley theatre lie three stone carvings one of which is the head of Ethelfleda. In 1972, when the council districts of Runcorn and Widnes merged, there was public debate for the new name of the district. Bridgetown was my favourite suggestion and many residents suggested the town could twin with their namesake in Jamaica and organise lots of cross Atlantic twin visits and meetings. I would have put my name down for the first flight for the inaugural twinning meeting in Jamaica. However, it was decided that the area should be called the not-so-glamorous name of Halton. Unfortunately, if you go to south Halton today you would realise that Bridgetown would have been such an appropriate name as there are now three bridges over the river Mersey. The Ethelfleda bridge (or Britannia rail bridge as it is now known) is situated alongside the Silver Jubilee road bridge (opened in 1961) which overlooks the £600 million, six lane, Mersey Gateway bridge (opened in 2017). The area that is affected the most by this trinity of bridges is south Widnes, called West Bank. It is an area that retains its sense of community and sense of humour even though it is encircled by the arterial routes to the three bridges and it is often likened, jokingly because of its name, to the Jordanian / Israeli border.

My curiosity in borders stems from an interest in travel. A student opportunity to go inter-railing through the whole of Europe in 1979 for only £89 was too exciting to miss. There were many long waits at border boundaries and there was an increase in my heartbeat as armed guards entered the train at Vigo on the Portugal/Spain border. After Spanish officials shouted their way up and down the carriages, the train would stutter to the next border station on the Portuguese side for the whole process to start again. We slept on the uncomfortable seats overnight as the train crossed many European borders, in order that we didn't have to pay for camping site accommodation. Once I fell asleep on the train travelling from Denmark to Norway, waking up in the middle of the night as the motion of the train went silently up and down rather than its usual rhythmic clickety-clackety rattle. I looked out of the train window only to realise that the train had driven onto a ferry and the movement was caused by the lurching of the ship. The Danish transport authority was very considerate, planning a system that did not wake up their rail passengers, so they could be transported on and off the ferry without disembarking the train.

After three weeks of European rail travel on what was left of the student grant, funds were seriously low (but at least at that time we did not have to pay the grant money back). A Rome experience should be forgotten where we had to run for a crowded bus as two of the group hastily stuffed their passports into their backpacks. Unsurprisingly, when we reached the train station, the passports had disappeared. This resulted for them in a trip to the British embassy and an early journey home to the UK. The remainder of the group travelled to Venice sleeping on the Lido beach rather than paying for a campsite. With our thirst for Italian culture satisfied, it was time to travel to a very different country that was called Yugoslavia: the home to the beguiling Tito communist regime. Surrounded by many armed police and army officials, our blue passports were scrutinised (I still maintain it was a black passport, but Brexit supporters insist that it is a shade of blue). We entered the train with a payment choice of either first class or third class seats, and yes this was an egalitarian communist state; wasn't everyone supposed to be equal? For all its faults, Yugoslavia was a wonderful blessing as it had superb beaches and, fortunately, it was the most affordable country in Europe at the time.

My interest in maps arises from geography lessons at school. One of my first recollections was a project, in pairs, to research an assigned country. My working partner was Jack, who was new to the school having arrived from Australia. I asked him if all his family had a criminal record? He seemed to have a good understanding of my sense of humour and we were good mates for the rest of our schooldays and beyond. I had not known anyone from the sunburnt country before and assumed he would be proficient at both rugby and cricket. It became obvious early on that this was not the case, and his geography skills seemed to be somewhat inaccurate as well. Our project involved researching the famous South American country called Bolivia. Not the most popular of countries and we duly churned out useless facts about its main exports and imports (no internet to Google in those days). What made us really laugh was when we realised that Queen Victoria had sent a fleet of ships to investigate Bolivia: only then did she realise that Bolivia was a landlocked country with not a coastline in sight. For further detail on Bolivia and South America see chapter seven. We stumbled upon an adolescent geography student's dream fact about the highest navigable lake in the world, which happened to be in our chosen country Bolivia. Of course, the answer was that the frontier between Bolivia and Peru bisects Lake Titicaca. We got our geography teacher to tell us the answer, several times, so that our fellow students could giggle when he said "titty".

My first geography teacher, Mr Williamson, asked if any student possessed an atlas at home? Foster, a conscientious student, raised his hand to reply that he had "an old, modern Philips atlas", to great laughter from the rest of the class. The changing nature of geography means that all atlases, as soon they are published, are out of date. Names change, rivers change course, landforms move, and sea levels rise. As Mark Monmonier writes "Maps are like milk:

their information is perishable and it is wise to check the date". (Monmoier 1996)

Borders can affect our everyday lives in many different ways. Different school half term holidays may not be the greatest problem to many people, however, if you live in Berwick-upon-Tweed and one offspring goes to a Scottish school and one child is educated at an English school, many school holidays are different, creating complex childcare issues.

Commonplace border crossings can be unnecessarily stressful. With two of my three daughters busy in a dance show, I took my youngest daughter and her best friend (Harriet) to Disneyland near Paris for a once in a lifetime trip. An uneventful drive down the M1 and M25 brought us to the car ferry and the Dover border guard station. Our travel documentation was valid, and all three passports were correct and in-date, always a relief. It was then that the border guard asked an unexpected question, "Sir, have you got written permission from Harriet's parents to take her out of the country?" There was no such undertaking and the faces of the two girls in the back seat were a picture of disappointment. I had never considered permission and had certainly never considered such an ignominious end to my teaching career, with headlines in the tabloid papers no doubt looking something like *Geography teacher in kidnapping and trafficking horror! Smuggles ten-year old girl into France in his car!* Fortunately, the most unusual thing happened at the border, as the guard used that quality so often lacking at frontiers – common sense. We were then allowed to board the ferry and were on our way to meeting Mickey, Baloo and Cruella De Vil.

Many people believe the concept of borders is a paradox: some borders trap us, others give us a sense of freedom. There is a need for both mobility and roots. "Among the great struggles of man" Salman Rushdie writes in *The Ground Beneath Her Feet*, "there is also this mighty conflict between the fantasy of Home and the fantasy of Away, the dream of roots and the mirage of journey". Some people have avoided the concept of the border by staying on residential ships, like "The World", that tour the earth or at least the oceans; other people just want to anchor to one particular place.

Borders of the mind can be unmapped and unseen but are the ones that affect our lives on a day-to-day basis. The shops visited, footpaths walked down, parks and towns investigated all have a sense of a line which we do not like to cross. Gang warfare has often depended on lines and places where you cannot go. The county lines of drug-dealers are just one example of division of place. There are other examples such as Glasgow in 1984 where six people died because of the turf war...between ice-cream vans.

Imaginary boundaries are insignificant compared with actual borders. Many international borders and borders within countries follow natural features such as mountains or rivers, especially in the continents of Africa, Australasia and North and South America. Where these features are absent, a ruler and use of a line of latitude or parallel would suffice to create a border sometimes over thousands of miles, causing many unintentional consequences. Europe has seen a thousand years of fighting over the drawing and fluidity of borders.

It would appear that very little has stayed the same regarding borders. This is illustrated by someone born in 1870 who lived into their late seventies and resided in the same Strasbourg house all their life: they would have changed nationality fully five times, being bounced like a ball between France and Germany (Parker 2010). Heads of state have repeatedly redrawn borders to the detriment of the residents involved. For instance, when Disraeli was involved in modifying the map of the Balkans at the Berlin Conference in 1878, apparently, he could not hold the map the right way up.

Simply, a definition of a border is a line or boundary separating two countries or areas. In reality it is so much more than this as it entices you to step over or cross the line. An actively policed border is nearly always aggressive, perhaps protecting a nationalist ideology. Bewilderingly, there are at least seventy border walls in the world today. According to Di Cintio in his book *Walls* "We are a species of claustrophobic travellers. Walls may define our borders, but they defy our nature". (Di Cintio 2016)

The British author Tolkien's most widely read works, *The Hobbit* and *The Lord of the Rings*, take place entirely in Middle-earth. This location has also become shorthand to refer to Tolkien's fictional take on the world. Frank Jacobs in the New York Times suggests:

> Tolkien might have done without borders on his map, but ours are richer for it. Tracing them across the globe, we find enclaves and exclaves, disputed and neutral zones, improbably straight and impossibly jagged borders, deadly borders born in war and old ones almost faded into irrelevance. And even if they coincide with rivers or mountain ranges, they remain entirely human constructs. They can be as wondrous, frightening and magical as anything in Middle-earth. (Jacobs 2011)

Bordering on the Ridiculous is not a travel book, as such, but a collection of my observations related to borders. It is more like a series of spectacular events of border history. Trying to see the lighter side of life, there are many examples of the quirky, weird and amazing stories that are incorporated with these border features. Often linked to the natural landscape, people have made recognised borders throughout history and not necessarily in the most obvious location. The book concentrates on the positive and humorous aspects of borders throughout the world, although I am fully aware of the hardship around various frontiers and barriers and these too are covered. Though these are important issues, it is not a book that tries to involve politics or contemplates migration and refugee issues.

CHAPTER 1
MINISTRY OF BARRIERS, WALLS AND FENCES

"I have always loved the moments of travel when, brought to a halt by a striped barrier, approached by unfamiliar uniforms, you feel yourself on the brink of somewhere unknown and possibly perilous."

JAN MORRIS, *TRIESTE AND THE MEANING OF NOWHERE* (2001; FOR MORE ON TRIESTE SEE CHAPTER FIVE).

James McCarthy removed his sun helmet and scratched his head thoughtfully. His hair was slick with perspiration. The air was sticky, and the grove of stunted papaya trees offered little in the way of shade. He was beginning to appreciate the magnitude of his assignment. Appointed by the King of Siam in 1880 to survey his dominion's borders (no, not Yul Brynner in the film *The King and I*), McCarthy seemed to be the only person interested in the task. Here, local elders told McCarthy that the border with British Burma was defined by two papaya trees, but they couldn't remember which ones. To the elders it wasn't important. They had left McCarthy in the hot sun to decide for himself.

Nineteenth-century ideas of clearly drawn boundaries were novel in many parts of the world, as they had been in Europe in earlier centuries. The King of Siam did not understand the significance of borders until the British started cutting down large areas of forest and building railways. Many places were under the influence of numerous authorities, and borders between adjacent kingdoms did not necessarily touch. For cartographers like McCarthy, it must have been difficult to map large unclaimed regions of forest and mountains (Middleton 2015).

Improvements in surveying and cartography and the desire of countries to carve up the world's surface into colonies has created diverse borders. These borders represent the "skin of the state" (Franck Bille suggested the borders-as-skin metaphor), the edge of a country's territorial control. Physically, borders define a modern country thereby playing an important symbolic role in identifying the nation. A world map shows assured lines separating countries suggesting that their citizens rule over every inch of their land. However, this is not necessarily the case as there are many exclaves and enclaves. An exclave is a slice of one country's territory not attached to the rest of it - it is surrounded entirely by another country. An enclave is territory that is surrounded totally by a foreign state.

There are many disputed territories in the world such as Transnistria in Moldava to name one (see chapter five). Many recognised countries have borders that have never been defined and agreed by a treaty, for example Cooch-Behar in India (see chapter six). Many nations have not had their borders delimited or actually marked on the ground such as the Saharan Sand Wall (see chapter seven). Clearly, the lack of agreement on borders can lead to long-running disputes such as in Kashmir (see chapter four). The situation with border recognition means that numerous countries come and go. Many states have endured, some have split into multi-nations, such as the former Yugoslavia, and some have been created like the most recent nation in the world, South Sudan.

When the United Nations publish maps they come with a more explicit caveat than a pack of cigarettes and do not imply "...the expression of any opinion whatsoever on the part of the Secretariat of the United Nations concerning the legal status of any country, territory, city or area or of its authorities, or concerning the delimitation of its frontiers or boundaries" (from United Nations OHCHR – Office of the High Commissioner for Human Rights). It is no wonder that nothing is set in concrete and that new or micronations see murky or ill-defined borders as an opportunity rather than a threat (for more on micronations see chapter seven).

There is a small village in south east Luxembourg on the western bank of the river Moselle near the tripoint where the borders of Germany, France and Luxembourg meet. This village, or commune as the locals call it, has a total population of only 4,223 but it has had a disproportionate major influence on European affairs (Wikipedia 2004). On a boat called the *Princess Marie-Astrid* on the river Moselle, five of ten member states signed an agreement on border controls. Why is this so important? Nothing to do with Prince Charles and his alleged romantic interest: the eldest daughter of the Grand Duke of Luxembourg, the gorgeous Princess Marie-Astrid (yes, I admit I had a crush on this princess back in 1976). The place is called Schengen. Perhaps this location is at the top of the list of small places that defy their influence on world events; I suggest its influence may be as important as Camp David, Davos and Bretton Woods. Since the five states, twenty-six European countries signed the Schengen Agreement removing passport control between its member countries, this means that travellers who go from one Schengen country to another do not clear immigration checks anymore. A brilliant idea that gives reassurance to many people. The Schengen concept is an exception because in many parts of Europe and throughout the rest of the world hard borders are still prevalent.

Winston Churchill is famous for his oration, and as leader of the opposition in 1946 (he had been voted out of office after the war victory in 1945) he announced a new boundary by describing it as follows: "From Stettin in the Baltic to Trieste in the Adriatic, an iron curtain has descended across the continent". The northern extent was Stettin which is the German place name and in Polish it is a seaport called Szczecin; the southern point was Trieste in Italy (see chapter five). This Iron Curtain was an ideological barrier between Soviet-controlled Eastern Europe and the West that gradually became a physical one spanning over 6,800 kilometres (4,200 miles). Effectively, it was the start of the Cold War which was a period of geopolitical tension between the Soviet Union (East) and the USA (West). To stop their citizens from fleeing to the West, the Soviet-dominated Eastern countries began erecting various forms of barriers using barbed wire, ditches and concrete walls. The partitions were controlled through alarms, watchtowers, mines and armed soldiers.

The Berlin Wall was the most famous section of the Iron Curtain and became its symbol of communist oppression. Many people who were stuck on the wrong side of this barrier developed ingenious ways to cross. One man crossed via a wire cable that was shot by a bow and arrow from the roof of a building to a relative's house on the other side. Others escaped by swimming across Berlin's Spree River or digging tunnels underneath the wall. A teacher friend brought me a present of a piece of blue painted concrete from her travels in Germany – an original piece of the Berlin Wall, or so she said, because it did look rather like a lump from a school playground. It provided the resource for many exciting geography lessons (yes, they do exist), together with an alleged stone from Hadrian's Wall and a lump from the Great Wall of China (I am not sure how that made it through customs).

Berlin Wall Museum (© Jorge Royan)

There are historic tube maps in Berlin showing how, in places, the underground railway was simply bricked up, sometimes through the night, as the city was divided between the East and West. There are ghost stations (called geisterbahnhofes) which are the U-Bahn and S-Bahn stops in the eastern sector that were on railway lines connecting different parts of the western zone. These stations were sealed, while armed Eastern guards (Ossi) made sure no one got on or off as the trains passed by. Some stations straddled the border, so that platforms and exits had to be divided or sealed. In a few places, there were parallel railway lines belonging to the two different halves, East and West, requiring large fences between them in case anyone jumped across from train to train. The legendary Checkpoint Charlie on Friedrichstrasse was named from the NATO phonetic alphabet (Alpha, Bravo, Charlie): after the border crossings at Helmstedt-Marienborn (Alpha) and Dreilinden-Drewitz (Bravo) were named, Checkpoint Charlie was the third checkpoint opened by the Allies in and around Berlin (hence the "C"). It became the most famous crossing point between East and West Germany. On 22 September 1961, East German guards began registering members of the American, British and French forces before they were able to organise trips to East Berlin. The checkpoint had become a designated crossing point for members of the Allied armed forces and a month later in October 1961 it became the scene of a tank confrontation. American and Soviet tanks took up position and faced each other with weapons primed. The potential for World War III was only averted when President John F. Kennedy contacted Soviet leader Nikita Khrushchev and convinced him to withdraw his tanks. A few minutes later, the American tanks also left the scene. It was the only gateway where East Germany allowed Allied diplomats, military personnel and foreign tourists to pass into Berlin's Soviet sector. In response, the United States, France and Britain stationed military police at Checkpoint Charlie to ensure their officials had ready access to the border. The Allied guards spent most of their time monitoring diplomatic and military traffic, but they were also on hand to register and provide information to travellers before they ventured beyond the Wall.

Checkpoint Charlie attracted many desperate East Germans looking to flee to the West. In April 1962, an Austrian named Heinz Meixner took his East German girlfriend, her mother and himself across the border by lowering the windshield on a rented Austin-Healey convertible and speeding underneath the checkpoint's vehicle barrier. Later in his life, I hope that he never regretted taking his future mother-in-law! The guardhouse was dismantled in 1989 and the original now sits on display at the Allied Museum in Berlin. A replica version of the guardhouse was later installed as a tourist attraction where tourists swarm to have their *selfie* taken with a fake American or Soviet soldier. Perhaps the best way to visit is via a *Segway* tour (see chapter seven) as a way to get you in and out of this crowded tourist hot spot as quickly as possible. The destruction of the Berlin Wall in November 1989 was the most graphic illustration, played out on many of our television screens, that division can be overcome. Fortunately, the East-West barrier only lasted for forty years, and the physical Berlin Wall remained for twenty-eight years. In that time, almost eighty people had died trying to cross the Wall and it had created tension and suffering amongst Berliners and even within families. In the late 1960s a German psychiatrist Dietfried Muller-Hegemann had noticed a spike in cases of despondency followed by bouts of excitement: a dentist waiting on the shores of the Baltic Sea for no apparent reason; a civil servant who claimed he was spied upon; a seamstress who thought lesbians were trailing her. They had something in common in that they all lived close to the Berlin wall. His book published in 1973 gave this syndrome a name "Mauerkrankheit" or wall disease (wall in the head).

When leaving Berlin today, Schönefeld airport has a reputation for strict security as Adam Fletcher highlights in his book *Don't Go There*. Although asked many questions by security staff, the most difficult were about his occupation. At airport security, you do not want to be labelled a journalist or a writer because of their habit of writing things that are true about a place. He was strip-searched, interrogated and his laptop was checked; well it did have a loose screen and a battery that was stuck in by Sellotape. Without a doubt, you do not want to be in possession of such an item if you are entering Ben Gurion airport in the security-conscious country of Israel. (Fletcher 2018)

So why did Mark Thomas, in his book *Extreme Rambling* (Thomas 2011), stick to the route walking along the barrier that is the West Bank wall? His wife replies "because he is shit at map reading!" A wall of grey slabs of concrete rise eight metres from the ground and are bound so tightly together that not a beam of sunlight reaches through. Floodlights, watchtowers and security cameras are displayed like a scene from Orwell's book *Big Brother*. (Thomas 2011). The Israeli West Bank barrier or wall is a separation barrier in the West Bank. The West Bank (which refers to the west bank area of the river Jordan) fell under Israeli control in 1967, after a combined assault by Syria, Egypt and Jordan had been repulsed in the Six-Day War. Curiously, although today many atlases used in Palestinian schools do not show the state of Israel, they refer to the arbitrary borders established by the armistice of 1949. This is done by showing the course of the Green Line. Israel calls it a security barrier against terrorism, while Palestinians call it a racial segregation or apartheid wall. At a total length of 708 kilometres (440 miles) upon completion, the route traced by this barrier is more than double the length of the Green Line (the armistice boundary drawn in 1949 and internationally accepted as the border between Israel and the West Bank). With 85% of the barrier length inside the West Bank going up to 18 kilometres (11 miles) from the West Bank border, it isolates about 9% of the land and 25,000 Palestinians from the rest of West Bank. The Wall divides Palestinian villages from both their farmland and neighbouring towns. By the way, the Wall is also illegal according to the International Court of Justice which issued an "Advisory Opinion" in 2004, concluding that the barrier's route breached human rights law. Many geographers argue that the security fence is an example of a border being built: in other words, it is a cartographic "fait accompli".

There are many positive stories from this region of residents who are defiant in the face of adversity. Al Aqaba village, for instance, is physically cut off, isolated in the mountains, and almost the entire village is under demolition orders. There is no surprise that the population has reduced from four hundred to one hundred and therefore its survival is threatened. Financial help has arrived from the United Nations and countries such as USA, Japan, Belgium, Netherlands, Denmark and Norway. Donations have helped to build a school, roads, wells and other infrastructure. The influence of the British is still in the region because Jack Straw, as UK foreign secretary from 2001 to 2006, stopped a demolition order by the Israelis for the medical clinic. At Tayba, the barrier cuts directly across the football pitch of the boys' school. So, some would suggest that if the Israelis ever want to stop the opposition from scoring a goal, they build an electric fence in front of the goal! In the village of Anin, farmers queue at dawn to pass through an agricultural crossing gate to get to their own land, now found on the other side of the wall. There is a large yellow sign attached to the gate that gives precise, if unhelpful instructions:

Gate number: BLANK. The passage through this gate will be permitted between the hours of BLANK. In case of emergency or a closed gate please ring **(yes you have guessed it)** *BLANK.* **(Thomas 2015)**

Banksy has a much clearer message in his *Walled Off* hotel graffiti art-work "Make Hummus, not Walls". He says it has "the worst view of any hotel in the world", while its 10 rooms get just 25 minutes of direct sunlight a day. However, nestled against the controversial wall, the West Bank's answer to the Waldorf hotel offers travellers something more elusive than any luxury destination. This lodging in Bethlehem is a hotel, museum, protest and gallery all rolled into one, packed with the artworks and angry brilliance of its owner, British street-artist 'Banksy'. One of my favourite photographs of Banksy artwork is called *Palestine* which says: "Visit Palestine - the Israeli army liked it so much they never left". Another special piece of graffiti is on a long and high stretch of the barrier written in massive, white letters. The humorous message consists of two simple words: "OPEN SESAME".

Mark Thomas (2011) writes about Alfei Menashe, an Israeli settlement with a military barrier surrounding it. It is inaccessible from the West Bank so to get there he left Palestine, entered Israel and then re-entered Palestine, or at least a part of it with settlers on. In a car he could tell which side of the barrier he was on even if he was blindfolded, as the lack of swerving and sudden braking indicated an absence of potholes which would place you on the Israeli side with certainty. However, he does recommend not to attempt any sort of blindfold experiment, as being blindfolded in a car in the West Bank has an altogether different connotation! Whereas Alfei Menashe is under Israeli law, the village of Arab ar Ramadin is under military law. Here, there is no electricity, the houses are not brick and 90% of them have demolition orders against them. If you drive a car to the checkpoint, the soldiers insist that all the passengers get out 300 metres before the checkpoint and then walk the 300 metres, while the driver goes through. The passengers are taken to a security room to be checked. Then they have to walk to the car on the other side. Perhaps this may be acceptable if you are fit and healthy, but this may not be the case for the elderly, pregnant or sick people possibly returning from hospital after surgery. This area is known as the Seam Zone (the area known for creating conditions so disruptive that the Palestinians think that enough is enough and decide to leave their lands).

The barrier does not only take up land but also water. The route of the barrier runs over the Western Aquifer, the main source of drinking water in the West Bank, denying Palestinians the ability to extract water from this vital underground source. As a result, the grass is, quite literally, greener on the Israeli side of the 'fence'.

On the other side of Road 443 is a village boys' school. For the Israelis planning the barrier they had to do three things. Firstly, they had to allow the barrier to surround the neighbouring Israeli settlement of Beit Horon, secondly to maintain an Israeli-only road, and thirdly to still allow the Palestinian children to cross to their school. The answer was simple enough - dig a tunnel under the road. The students walk from the village to the hillside, scramble down a dirt track, walk along the edge of Road 443 and take a stone stairway down to the tunnel that leads under the road. This is not a well-maintained underpass like the tunnel in Woolwich under the river Thames. There are no tiles, murals, or even lights, just a dark and small concrete hole, less glamorous than a drain. The tunnel is divided in half by two narrow channels. The one raised slightly above the other is where the children walk. No one walks in the lower channel because it is for drainage and when it rains sewage comes down from the settlement. To make matters worse, the Israeli army have placed a demolition order on the school toilets. As Mark Thomas (2011) suggests "Apparently, the Israeli authorities are happy for the kids to walk in a tunnel next to human shit but not to let them have a toilet".

The Wall makes healthcare complicated in this region because the hospitals are far away and it is sometimes difficult to cross the barrier. As a result, Palestine is the only place in the world that has three sets of statistics for childbirth – home births, hospital births… and births at checkpoints! The Wall inevitably has spurned a tourist industry where there are many different tours to see evidence of the three religions of the Holy City (Old and New Jerusalem), biblical tours and even a tour of Wall graffiti. Perhaps one of the most interesting would be a dual narrative tour of Hebron (Moore 2016). The morning is led by an Israeli guide and the afternoon led by a Palestinian student guide. The tour bus is much like any other in the world except for the fact that the driver carries a revolver on his hip and all the windows are bullet proof.

Inevitably, there are tourist shops and street sellers. Near the Wailing Wall in Jerusalem, there is a clothes seller who advertises shawls with the slogan "the prayer shawl you've been praying for". Mentioning clothes reminds me of a story concerning Yasser Arafat (Palestinian political leader) who once claimed that he spent an hour every day folding his "Keffiyeh" head dress so that it would resemble a map of his longed-for Palestine State. Presumably, he was trying to show to everyone that Palestine was quite literally on his mind! (Jacoby 2009)

Mark Thomas (2011) asks a telling question to an Israeli Zionist estate agent, "If God promised you all this land, and He wants you to have it, why did He put all these Arabs in the way?" He also tells the story of musician Odeh Salameh, a tall figure of a man who sways from side to side like Ray Charles when he sings. Odeh's problem is with official maps and boundaries (not the only person who has this problem). Between two buildings lay the Jerusalem municipal boundary so that the Wall went over the doorstep to his resident apartments, trapping a small part of Jerusalem on the West bank side of the Wall. The result is that his living room and part of the dining room are in Jerusalem because they are over the municipal line; the rest of the apartment (the toilet, kitchen and bedrooms) are in the West Bank. Therefore, part of Odeh's home is in Israel, but he only has a West Bank ID card. The police and army have raided Odeh's home saying his family need permission to enter Israel, in other words to use their own living room. He was arrested and put on a computer list to say he had entered Israel illegally. This meant he could not go to work in Jerusalem. He paid an expensive lawyer to be able to receive a permit to go to work. To go to the toilet in Odeh's house you leave the living room in Israel, enter the West Bank to use the facility, re-enter Israel via the dining room, go into the West Bank at the stairwell, return to Israel at the doorsteps and are then back in the West Bank. As *Tears for Fears* would sing, it really is a "Mad World".

There are few places more frozen in time than Nicosia and the UN-patrolled buffer zone in Cyprus. In that space of barbed wire, sandbags and guard posts, there is no place that conjures up more division than the Ledra Palace hotel. It was once a magnet for Hollywood stars such as Elizabeth Taylor and Richard Burton, famed as much for its ballroom as its invention of the brandy sour. The marble-topped bar was tended by a famous barman who apparently invented the brandy sour for Egypt's King Farouk. If there were devout Muslims in this king's company, he would want a drink that was disguised as a fruit juice. It became the unofficial cocktail of Cyprus. I had to do the 'drinking research' in order to discover that it contains brandy, lemon, bitters and soda water. Although the drink may have been a success, the hotel has come to symbolise the failure of peace envoys, diplomats and politicians to reunite Europe's last divided capital, Nicosia. The bullet and rocket-scarred facade, like its shattered chandeliers, demonstrate the conflict that has split this beautiful island between Greeks and Turks since 1974 (Di Cintio 2012). A line was drawn on a map of Cyprus to divide the two parties commonly known as the "Green Line" and the UN Buffer Zone was set up to keep the two sides apart.

Moving to the coast of Cyprus and there should be a warm welcome in Varosha, the Mediterranean's best kept secret. Here, there are miles of golden sand where there is just you and nature. There are dozens of grand hotels where you will have the pick of the rooms. You will not have seen it on Tripadvisor or in a tourist brochure and you will need to remember to pack your bolt cutters to make a hole in the fence around Varosha. Also, you may want to watch out for the army patrols which have orders to shoot on sight. Before the division of Cyprus in 1974, Varosha, a resort in the region of Famagusta, was booming. The rich and famous such as Brigitte Bardot were drawn by some of the finest beaches on the island and the best hotels, such as the Argo Hotel on JFK Avenue. Locals talked about it being the hub of art and intellectual activity, although Peter Andre was nowhere to be seen! They described it as the French Riviera of Cyprus. As Turkish troops approached Varosha by boat for the invasion in 1974, the inhabitants (Greek-Cypriots) fled intending to return when the situation calmed down. However, the resort was fenced off by the Turkish military and it has been a ghost town ever since. (Smith 2019)

I stayed in Kapparis, a small tourist resort with beaches where you could swim out to almost within reach of North Cyprus. I wondered what had happened to the wildlife when the Turks invaded it and the Green Line was installed. I realised that plants reach out across this border, uninterested in the lines that people trace over maps and the barriers they build. The zoo animals, roaming around the Buffer Zone because their cages were damaged, ended up in a makeshift zoo. The zoo buildings and cages are overlooked by a tower which I can recommend climbing, because they reveal the best secret views of the UN Buffer Zone and look over to Famagusta in the north. A strange zoo on a road to nowhere that would have continued to North Cyprus except for the buffer zone. If you want a property investment that may increase in value overnight this is the area to invest; alas it relies on North Cyprus, South Cyprus, Greek and British parties all agreeing a settlement. They have been talking about this agreement since the 1974 invasion, so I am sure there is more profitable real estate available elsewhere.

I boarded a red London double-decker bus outside the accommodation in Kapparis and headed to cross the UN Buffer

Zone, the "Green Line", with EU passport in hand. In 2003, travel restrictions were eased for the first time, allowing Cypriots and tourists on both sides daily to cross the UN Buffer Zone. A tourist company had shown great initiative and had imported London buses and set up cross-border trips. A fascinating crossing over the Green Line and a completely different country emerged. Coffee for instance was a third of the price and clothing souvenirs had a Middle Eastern theme. Signs warned tourists about peering across the fence and that "photos and movies are forbidden." Simply, trespassers risk death. Some exiled residents have regularly pinned love-letters and flowers to the barbed wire in memory of the glory of Varosha. Other than the Turkish soldiers, few people have ventured inside this town. Those that have, describe extraordinary sights such as a car dealership still stocked with 1974 cars, window displays of mannequins dressed in long-gone fashions, the sand dunes that have encroached over the seafront with rare sea turtles nesting in them. Some pictures of the desolation circulate online but the photographers won't always admit to taking them, perhaps for obvious reasons.

Back to Nicosia, I crossed the buffer zone in the middle of the capital city observing the shelled buildings, bullet-holed walls and sandbags. Again, on the Turkish side the shops sold cheaper items of clothes, food and drink. Another bullet-scarred structure came into view. The building was a UN border post originally manned by Canadian forces who named it, patriotically, Maple House. It occupied the second floor above what had once been a Toyota dealership (similar to the one in Varosha). The shop had been shuttered since the 1974 invasion, but it is claimed that there is an inventory of "brand new" 40 plus year old Toyotas still occupied in a basement showroom. Their odometers read only sixty miles, the distance from the port of Famagusta, where they arrived, to this dealership. If you pass Maple House into the Buffer Zone and go across an abandoned schoolyard marked with faded football boundaries, there is a derelict yellow sedan standing on blocks. A sign on the car declares, somewhat obviously, "Yellow Car".

Apparently, the car was an official UN observation post. When the buffer zone was first marked out by the UN in 1974, the peacekeepers described the Turkish-Cypriot territory at this point as extending from the front of the abandoned car to the corner of a nearby building. The Turkish military, however, debated the definition of front. The UN took "front" to mean the car's headlights and accordingly drew the line from there. The Turks, however, felt that the "front" of the car in this case was the part of the car closest to the next border post. This meant the Turks would gain a small plot of extra territory if the line was drawn this way. They settled on a quirky compromise as the Turks accepted the UN's meaning of front, but as an expression of their authority over the area, a Turkish soldier stands next to the car for 5 minutes every hour (Di Cintio 2012).

I spent longer than anticipated on the fascinating Turkish side of Nicosia and decided to walk back through the Ledra Palace border crossing approaching dusk. An eerie silence fell upon the Buffer Zone as I showed my passport to the Turkish border guards. Two hundred metres to cross back to the southern Greek part of Cyprus – it could have been two hundred miles, as the photographs of freedom fighters were highlighted on pictures that were pinned to notice boards. Perhaps dusk was not the most sensible time of day to return. I remembered a story from an ex British officer who recalled an army man in Cyprus who parachuted from an aeroplane, but his false leg fell off over the other side of the Green Line. He decided that it was quicker to have a new artificial leg manufactured than to obtain permission from the Turkish authorities to go over the border to collect it (note this story not substantiated by the British army).

In February 1848, the border between the U.S. and Mexico originated with the signing of the Treaty of Guadalupe Hidalgo. A 3,200-kilometre (2,000 mile) line on a map between the two countries ended a bitter war. This border begins at the Pacific Ocean dissecting the beach between San Diego and Tijuana. The line separates California from Baja California and divides the Sonoran

Desert in Arizona and covertly moves half-way across New Mexico. At El Paso in Texas, the border merges with the middle of the Rio Grande. This river then becomes the border for the final 2,000-kilometre line across the North American continent until it flows into the Gulf of Mexico. Up until the 1990s, the border remained as rolled-out barbed wire and the occasional stone. In 2006, President George W. Bush signed the Secure Fence Act in response to the vulnerability Americans felt in the wake of the September 11th attacks (even though none of the hijackers infiltrated the U.S. through a land border). President Trump continued the high-profile wall building. However, although 645 kilometres (400 miles) of wall were built under Trump's four years at the White House, only nine miles of the construction were new parts of the wall. The remainder were replacing old or broken barriers.

Highway I-19 usually has road signs in miles like the rest of USA. This highway links Tucson with the border at Nogales and the road signs are painted, with consideration, in kilometres for the drivers who are from Mexico. Unfortunately, any goodwill stops there. In the 1990s, the U.S. border control erected a barrier wall out of "helicopter landing mats" to cut off Nogales in Arizona from Nogales in Sonora. This physical border stopped lots of activities between the towns, but not all. As an example, Charles Mingus, the famous jazz musician, was born on the American side of Nogales but played the double bass in jazz clubs on both sides of the border. Ironically his army father was originally stationed there to stop illegal crossings! For another musician, Glenn Weyant, the wall itself is a musical instrument. He can attach a microphone to a steel panel to an amplifier and play the wall:

"Glenn danced his fingers over the steel panels as if trying to tap the cold reptilian veins. Tiny booms and buzzes echoed out of the amplifier. The sounds crossed the dusty border road and floated up the hill where National Guard troops and Border Patrol agents stared, bewildered, at a plaid-shirted man fondling the border they were charged to protect." (Di Cintio 2012).

Of course plugging microphones into a set of headphones and

fastening it to a metal wall, must have looked like a very suspicious act. If he was discovered near the wall, it would have taken a lot of explaining to the authorities who may have believed that he was there to destroy it, not play it!

The desperation of many Mexican immigrants to enter the United States means that they are willing to take drastic measures to get past border patrol officers. While this normally means overcoming border points, climbing over fences or even digging elaborate tunnels, others have found more elaborate methods. In 2001, Enrique Aguilar Canchola went a step further by attempting to sew himself into a seat in a car that was driven through a checkpoint. Canchola was caught because agents working at the border are used to having to inspect vehicles very carefully. They will often perform scans on cars and lorries passing through to search for immigrants and drugs. On previous occasions the authorities have found people hiding inside engine compartments and even in door panels!

The new barrier was not built all the way to the Pacific Ocean and the row of steel posts on the beach became a meeting point, known as Friendship Park, for people from both sides of the border. Relatives, without the correct paperwork to cross the border, set out deckchairs on the sand to talk to their loved ones across the border line in the U.S.A. Hands and fingers touched; romantic kisses were exchanged across the fence posts until this intimacy ended in 2008 when the Secure Fence Act built a new fifteen feet tall steel barrier on the beach creating a no man's land between the wall and the steel panels. This wall robbed the border of what little remained of its humanity and locals suggest it is now more like a dog pound. A religious mass used to be celebrated on the thick white sand of the beach with communion bread posted through the fence posts. This wafer (bread) transfer was stopped by Border Guards with helmets and flak jackets which was, perhaps, an overreaction against a reverend armed with a chalice full of holy wafers. After this confrontation, choirs sang hymns together on both sides of the border. The reverend declared that he was in the service of a greater power than the Department of Homeland Security as he walked past the agents to the wall. He was handcuffed and led away, only to be released later without charge. The Friendship Park reopened in 2012, after a backlash from activists. So now, every Saturday and Sunday, from 10:00 a.m. to 2:00 p.m., the United States Border Patrol allows people to enter the heavily supervised area. Though visitors can enter the outer fence, a second barrier of solid, steel-mesh blocks stops them from crossing over to the other side. Visitors on either side may look, talk, and listen, but touching is no longer an option. The fences make it impossible for people on opposite sides to embrace one another. The only physical contact anyone can hope for is perhaps the sad brush of a finger slipped through one of the small gaps. However, the good news is that people can now pray together. On Sundays, at the same time two pastors from the Border Church hold a religious service on opposite sides of the fence. It's a rare opportunity for families and friends across the divide to come together in song and prayer.

Reunion fence US Mexico border (Flickr.com)

Smuggling goods as well as people hit the headlines in 2020, when authorities found the longest ever smuggling tunnel stretching for 1,313 metres (4,309 feet): the tunnel had a lift, rail track, drainage and air ventilation systems, and high voltage electrical cables. The passageway connected an industrial site in the Mexican city of Tijuana to the San Diego area in California. In 2018, US authorities found a secret drug tunnel stretching from a former KFC in the state of Arizona to Mexico.

The environmental effect of the wall is noticeable as it cuts jaguar territory into two parts. The solution that the Department of Homeland Security engineers came up with was to cut small openings at the base of the border wall at regular intervals. These cat flaps were meant to allow the migrations of jaguars: although there has been a facetious suggestion that leaflets have been printed in both Spanish and English in order to tell the jaguars where the cat doors are located. The wall also interferes with the migration of Mexican grey wolves, Sonoran pronghorns (often mistakenly called an American antelope) and black bears. The wall prevents Mexican ocelots from breeding with south Texas mates (unless they work out the password for Tinder). The steel barrier is so imposing that pygmy owls, the smallest owls in the world, do not fly over it (even though physically they are capable). So, it appears that humans and wildlife have suffered from the building of the wall, with Black Hawks (helicopters) replacing red hawks in the skies around the border wall!

There are many different answers to the question asking what constitutes a weird tourist attraction. Some suggestions might be: a hot spring where you can swim in a hot tub of ramen (noodle soup, Japan); a Toilet Theme Park (South Korea); or where you can see a twenty metre wall full of used bubble gum (USA). There is another example called Parque Eco Alberto, where visitors can experience what it is like to illegally cross the border that separates Mexico from the United States. It involves a four-hour night hike through the rugged countryside with only a coyote-like guide to lead the way. There is no actual border and no laws are broken, but the landscape and experience are recreated as realistically as possible, including moving quickly on difficult tracks through unfamiliar areas. There may be 'predators' along the route that include both nature and man, as the "border crossers" are periodically instructed to hide from authorities and join together to stay safe. Although it takes place with a certain sense of humour, this is no publicity stunt. The park is operated by the local Native American community, the Hñahñus, and their objective is to teach the powerful lesson that border crossing is not safe, not fun, and not good for the local community (Di Cintio 2012).

The border can have some positive economic effects for both the USA and Mexico. The billboards that line the stretch of California's Interstate 8 highway towards Los Algodones make it clear travellers are not on their way to a typical tourism destination. The signs that beckon Americans as they head west toward Andrade, California's narrow border crossing, aren't for resorts or beaches but for dental clinics offering bridges and root canals at half what they cost in the United States. Dental care has become big business in Los Algodones over the last two decades, so much so that American visitors have nicknamed it "Molar City." An estimated 600 dentists operate out of hundreds of clinics that fill the small one square-mile town, which is home to fewer than 5,000 permanent residents (Di Cintio 2012).

"England under attack!" might be a headline from an imaginary newspaper in the eighth century. The attack was by Viking raiders, from Scandinavia and Denmark, who were related by both blood and language to the Anglo-Saxons. There was a large, uncoordinated and mysterious expansion by this multi-named group variously known as Norseman, Danes or Vikings. Their name would not have been important to the farmers, monks and raped women who suffered from their horrible fate. It was not just Britain that was pillaged by this group: there was also France, Iceland, Ireland, Greenland and parts of North America. At first, there were smash-and-grab raids along the east coast such as the monastery on Holy Island (Lindisfarne) in AD 793. The raids stopped for about 50 years, although this is where the cliché "calm before the storm" could be effectively used (Bryson 1990). In the year AD 850, over 350 Viking ships sailed up the river Thames instigating a series of battles across Britain. However, after an English battle win in AD 878, a treaty was signed establishing the Danelaw, a line (possibly could be described as a border) running between the English in the south and the Danes in the north. The area occupied by the Danelaw was approximately the area to the north of a line drawn between London and Chester, excluding the area of Northumbria to the east of the Pennines. Even today, it is an important dividing line between northern and southern dialects.

Map 1

After Barber 1993:129

There was a massive influence by the Danes in the north as can be seen from over 1,400 place names that are Scandinavian in origin such as Whitby, Scunthorpe, Skipton and I have to include Armthorpe, now the site for an Ikea distribution centre! Some people spoke Old English whereas in the next valley they may have only spoken Old Norse. However, generally there was a linguistic merger across the Danelaw line. Adopted Scandinavian terms such as freckle, skull, rotten, crawl, husband and sky replaced English words. Some argue it is still happening today with Ikea replacing some English words for furniture (many people know a Poang, Billy bookcase etc)! Many words stayed alongside each other, such as raise and rear, wish and want, craft and skill, ditch and dyke (see Offa's Dyke below). Unusually, the English even adopted Scandinavian pronouns such as 'they', 'them' and 'their'. So, an imaginary line (such as the Danelaw line) rather than a physical border can have a deep effect on the language of a country.

However, a large linear earthwork, named after Offa the Anglo-Saxon king of Mercia from AD 757 to 796, had a profound effect. Offa's Dyke (Welsh Clawdd Offa) originally delineated the border between Anglian Mercia and the Welsh kingdom of Powys. This structure was up to twenty metres wide and even eight metres high in places with a gulf-like ditch on its western side, roughly following the border between England and Wales (Crane 2016). Today, it is a protected monument running from Liverpool bay in the north to the Severn estuary in the south. The claim in AD 893 that this dyke ran "from sea to sea" may well have been Saxon hyperbole, but it still had a profound effect on our shores (Wikipedia 2004). The dyke that was forced on local people dissected woodland that was a valuable resource for charcoal burning, game and pannage (pig rearing). The ditch and earth bank diverted streams and run-off to change the drainage systems. Ancient trading routes along east-west lines that had carried goods for centuries were blocked by the north-south bank and ditch. The earthwork hardened an emerging internal border within Britain and possibly fuelled the understandable rivalry between Welsh and English people.

Another physical but natural border between Wales and England is the River Severn. Communication between the two countries improved when the Severn Bridge (Welsh: Pont Hafren) was built in 1966. It is a motorway suspension bridge that spans the River Severn and River Wye between Aust in Gloucestershire, England and Chepstow in Monmouthshire, south-east Wales. The Second Severn Crossing opened in 1996, now called the Prince of Wales bridge, and improved links even more by taking the M4 motorway over the River Severn. A toll was collected on the English side, but only for vehicles travelling westwards from England to Wales. Drivers described it as a "tax on entering Wales" and this was not necessarily in jest! Originally, tolls were charged in both directions, but the arrangements were changed in the early 1990s to eliminate the need for a set of toll booths for each direction of travel. In December 2018, all toll lanes were permanently closed, officially marking the start of a toll-free journey into Wales for the first time since the bridge's construction, much to the delight of the television star couple Gavin and Stacey.

The Welsh border may be an invisible line today, but it is important for places such as Hay-on-Wye, the famous book town, which lies on the Welsh side of the border in the County of Powys. Although, as far as the Royal Mail is concerned, it is better, apparently, to use the County of Herefordshire for letters (the spelling is not to be confused with the county of Hertfordshire about 150 miles/240 kilometres away). With a mail service like that, it is no wonder why people send more and more emails! On April 1, 1977, bibliophile Richard Booth declared the Welsh town of Hay-on-Wye an independent kingdom with himself as its monarch. The town subsequently developed a healthy tourism industry based on literary interests, and "King Richard" (whose sceptre was a repurposed toilet plunger) awarded Hay-on-Wye peerages and honours to anyone prepared to pay for them. Surely, the clue to this story is the date in April that he declared independence! (For more about micronations see chapter seven).

There is another example of an informal partition in Wales. The Landsker line represents the boundary between the largely Welsh-speaking and largely English-speaking people in Pembrokeshire and Carmarthenshire. This line has been given an unfortunate name, because Landsker is the Norse word for frontier. However, there is no permanent boundary here. Many would better describe it is an informal border.

There is at least one border in England that may be classed as informal but the boundary between Lancashire and Yorkshire is viewed by many as a cultural fault line (Armitage 1998). The Colne Valley, in the white rose county of West Yorkshire, contains the last set of villages on the trans-pennine A62 road. Over the hill is Saddleworth, in the red rose county of Lancashire. Saddleworth used to be in Yorkshire but the Boundary Commission recognised how the land drained the rivers (the watershed) and changed it to Lancashire. One day a sign appeared at the brow of the hill with "Oldham Metropolitan Borough" in luminous green letters. The day after the sign was positioned, it was obliterated with a shotgun and replaced by a hand painted sign with a white rose. Every time the council replaced the sign, the white rose was back. This went on for months until the council gave up. Today, both signs are next to each other creating a sort of "war of the roses no man's land" (Armitage 1998). People setting off into Saddleworth for the day even talk about "going over the top" – as if they shouldn't necessarily be expected back! This cultural divide is often exaggerated by the local newspapers. One such headline ran as "Batting for Yorkshire" and it was not in the sports section. According to a scientist, pipistrelle bats from Yorkshire have a different dialect than Lancashire bats. The scientist added, by way of an explanation, that bats have a separate vocabulary and also talk in different frequencies. To locals this is no surprise, as the way people speak in the next village 'over the top', only five miles away, might as well be in France, or worse still in Cumbria! Of course, the red and white rose is not the only example of cultural divide. There is a pub called the "White Post" on Rimpton Hill that straddles the border of Dorset and Somerset. The county boundary runs right through the middle of the bar. When Dorset and Somerset had different licensing laws, people had to move from one side of the room to the other at 10pm in order to continue to drink legally until 10.30pm. "So when it was drinking up time in Dorset, customers would simply move to the other side of the public house in Somerset with longer drinking hours" (Bryson 2015).

Lundy is the largest island in the Bristol Channel. It lies 10 nautical miles, 19 kilometres, off the coast of Devon. Lundy gives its name to a British sea area and is one of the islands of England. In a 2005 opinion poll of *Radio Times* readers, Lundy was named as Britain's tenth greatest natural wonder. In 1924 Martin Harman bought the island and proclaimed himself king. Harman issued two coins of Half Puffin and One Puffin denominations in 1929, nominally equivalent to the British halfpenny and penny, resulting in his prosecution under the United Kingdom's Coinage Act of 1870. The House of Lords found him guilty in 1931, and he was fined £5 with costs. The coins were withdrawn and became collectors' items. Residents did not pay taxes to the United Kingdom and had to pass through customs when they travelled to and from Lundy Island. Although the island was ruled as a virtual fiefdom, its owner never claimed to be independent of the United Kingdom, in contrast to later territorial micronations (see chapter seven). In 1969 Jack Hayward, a British millionaire, purchased the island for £150,000 and gave it to the National Trust who leased it to the Landmark Trust. The Landmark Trust has managed the island since then, deriving its income from arranging day trips, letting out holiday cottages and from donations. They culled the rats that were eating bird eggs, so that the bird population has increased three-fold. Crime is not a problem on this island. A stolen fishing rod is the only recorded offence in the last five years. No one has been caught but the case is not closed, and all lines are open to the police.

Visiting the Geevor Mine museum in south-west England, one could imagine the hard conditions of the tin miners in this part of the country. However, the food the tin miners ate has been a source of border pride and protection against illness for hundreds of years. Few meals have roots as deep as the Cornish pasty, a hand-held meat and vegetable pie developed as a lunch for workers in this ancient English tin mining region. It has a characteristic semi-circular shape and an insulating crust which can also be used as a handle. This humble pasty is loved by many especially in the food town of Padstowe but, perhaps unfortunately, it rhymes with "nasty" rather than "tasty". It has received special designation, along with such other delicacies as Parma ham, Stilton and Champagne, as a protected regional food by the European Union. The Cornish pasty comes from a broader family of medieval English meat pies where the pastry was not eaten but was used to cook the meat inside. Tin miners' hands were often covered with arsenic-laden dust, so the crust could function as a disposable handle, rather than being eaten. Since 2011 the European Union's rules for what constitutes a true Cornish pasty have been much more restrictive than before 2011: to be a Cornish pasty, you must have potato, swede, onion and beef, with the filling containing at least 25 per cent vegetables and at least 12.5 per cent meat. Most importantly, the pasty was given 'protected geographical indication status' (PGI) and must be made in Cornwall and nowhere else. Cornish tradition, though, may allow for a little more variety because, according to a traditional Cornish tale "the devil never dared to cross the Tamar River from Devon to Cornwall for fear of the Cornish women's habit of putting anything and everything into a pasty *(Wikipedia* 2004).

Food rivalry and culture are even more evident in an afternoon tea delicacy. The culture of scones (the pronunciation of the word itself could spawn another book) is open to serious argument as The Devonian, or Devonshire, method is to split the scone in two, cover each half with clotted cream, and then add strawberry jam on top. However, in the Cornish method the warm 'scone' or 'bread split' is first split in two, then spread with strawberry jam, and finally topped with a spoonful of clotted cream. The choice is yours!

Much further north, by separating the 'barbarians' from the Romans, Hadrian divided the island of Britain with a wall after his visit to Britain in AD 122. He did not, as many people believe, separate Scotland from England because Hadrian's Wall is fully sixty-eight miles south of the border. He chose the most obvious geographical point: the sixty-mile constriction between the estuary of the Solway in the west to the mouth of the River Tyne in the east. As with the building of many walls, Hadrian's Wall cut communities in two, both ethnically and politically. Hadrian employed surveyors who used rivers, crags and volcanic intrusions to strengthen the wall. Local raw materials such as Dolerite stone, timber and turf were also used to build the wall and labour was provided by the three Roman legions in Britain. Along its entire seventy-three mile extent, gates were to be set at one-mile intervals, with two observation towers or turrets between one gate and the next. Before Hadrian's Wall was completed, it was decided that a much larger garrison was needed than could be accommodated in the gates and turrets. As a result, forts were built astride the wall with gates to the north and south so that units on either side had secure bases to make offensive forays in both directions. Evidently, the perceived threat was equally dangerous to the north and south. A second modification was the excavation of a deep ditch with two banks on either side, set back on the south side of the wall. This massive "vallum" meant that the number of crossing points was reduced from eighty to about sixteen and so the passage of people through the wall could be tightly controlled. For indigenous Britons, crossing from north to south was a distant memory and Emperor Hadrian's long wall was classified as a great success (by the Romans at least). Within months of Hadrian's death in AD 138, there was an attempt by Antoninus Pius to move the zone of control a hundred miles further north, with the building of another linear barrier. This time it was between the firths of Clyde and Forth requiring the digging of a huge ditch with a large bank and turf rampart on its northern side. The rampart itself stripped four hundred hectares of turf from the natural landscape. It was one wall too far. It was virtually abandoned eight years after completion and when the new emperor in Rome, Marcus Aurelius came to power, he ensured that the garrisons were back on Hadrian's Wall (Crane 2016).

A visit to the area where one of the oldest borders originated is essential to a border enthusiast. Arguably, the oldest border is set down after the Battle of Carham (circa 1018) where Uhtred, Earl of the Northumbrians, fought and lost to the combined forces of Malcolm II of Scotland and Owen the Bald (the King of Strathclyde). The battle determined a border approximately one mile long, running along the river Tweed between Berwick and Kelso. Today this border runs between Scotland and England down the middle of the river Tweed. The border makes an unusual change of direction between Coldstream and Wark because two acres of Scottish meadow are enclosed south of the border. The change of direction is not because of the Battle of Carham but as a result from a game of "Ba"! It is said locally that the men of Coldstream and the men at Wark play "Ba" (a game of mob football where the ball is manhandled towards the goal) and the winning side would claim Ba Green for their country. As Coldstream grew to have a larger population than Wark, the Coldstream men always won so the land became a permanent part of Scotland, but of course it was on the southern bank of the Tweed border.

One of the oldest bridges across the river Tweed is the Union Suspension Bridge, known locally as the Union Chain Bridge. It opened in 1820 as the longest wrought-iron suspension bridge in the world with a span of 137 metres and is the longest vehicular bridge of its type in the UK. The bar link construction was invented by Captain Samuel Brown who tested the bridge in a curricle (two wheeled carriage), towing twelve carts, before a crowd of 700 spectators. Today the old bridge needs strengthening and if you want to travel by car between the two countries you have to make sure there are not more than two cars on the bridge at any one time.

If you are ever travelling to Scotland from England it is much safer and quicker to go via the A1 road bridge!

Me, visiting The Union Chain Bridge across the River Tweed, Northumderland

There was a time on the Scottish Borders when people owed their tribal or clan loyalty to their blood relatives or families and it was common for these families to straddle the border. I have a friend whose maiden name was Reiver. The relevance of that fact here is that reiving refers to raiding or plundering of livestock along the Scottish and English borders. The Reiver rode a small sturdy pony known as a hobbler, which was noted for its ability to cover great distances over difficult ground at high speed. The Reiver would wear a steel bonnet and a quilted jacket made of stout leather sewn with plates of metal or horn to protect his body. Although the Reiver carried a variety of weapons including sword, dagger and axe, his preferred weapon was the 'lang spear' or border lance.

Berwick upon Tweed, the most northerly town in England, has

glamourised the concept of borders for years, changing hands between England and Scotland no less than thirteen times. Emotions run high in the area; artist Wendy Wood in 1950, for instance, moved the border sign south of the bank to the middle of the river Tweed. An interesting place to stay, Berwick upon Tweed is the home of Berwick Rangers Football Club. The club's notoriety comes not from its football prowess but because it is the only English team to have played in the Scottish league. Of course, it should not be confused with the town of North Berwick which is in Scotland (and plays in the Scottish league as well). Until relegation from the Scottish Football league in 2019, Berwick Rangers were among only a handful of teams in the world to play in a national football league other than their own country's league. Nobody is sure that, in the very unlikely event they played in the Scottish Premier league, they would be allowed to play in a European competition. Berwick's status as a club physically located in England led to the anomaly of them being the only team in the Scottish leagues who were subject to the implementation of the Taylor report following the tragic Hillsborough disaster in 1989.

Two nights in Berwick upon Tweed in two B&Bs led to different quirky experiences. The first one was a pleasant stone building with breakfast served on a table in the bedroom so, quite literally, a bed and a breakfast. When I first enter any accommodation, I make a mental note of where the fire exits are, just in case. I noted that at this B&B there was a sign which reassuringly said; "fire exit – walk out the front door". The next night's B&B was even quirkier. My Alfa Romeo eased down the drive to the car park on the north side of the river Tweed, beneath the Royal Border Bridge, which formed the last link on the east coast railway connection between London and Edinburgh. This impressive viaduct consisted of 28 arches built on a curve designed by Robert Stephenson in 1847. I thought that this was such an impressive location for a B&B car park, except that there was very limited space to park because there appeared to be 3 torpedoes taking up many of the car park spaces. I always adhere to the regulations for disabled and child / family spaces, but this really was stretching those rules. With trepidation, I parked my black Italian-styled car next to one of the torpedoes and booked in. A half hour comprehensive checking in ceremony from the sweet landlady ensued whilst looking out at a most picturesque view of the river and viaduct, but no mention of the torpedoes. I plucked up enough courage to ask if I was to sleep in close-proximity to three bombs that could blow several Clyde-built frigates out of the water. There was a simple explanation, of course, the metal objects were not torpedoes but fuel tanks from the recently decommissioned Tornado jets, bought off *eBay* I think. So, my mind was beginning to ease, until the proprietor mentioned that one of the tanks was still full of aircraft fuel! A walk around the town revealed a creative LS Lowry trail and a notice that told visitors the fascinating fact that the lighthouse took 20 gallons of paint to repaint it. B&Q missed out on the advertising for that fact. Fortunately, we were not at war at the time I visited the town, although I learnt that I had only just missed out on the war! In 1854, Queen Victoria declared war on Russia at the outbreak of the Crimean War in the name of Britain, Ireland, Berwick upon Tweed and all British Dominions. The town at the time was in one of those maddening phases where it didn't know which country it was in. When the Paris peace treaty was signed two years later in 1856, it omitted Berwick which was quite an important administrative error. So officially it was at war with Russia until someone noticed the error in 1961 when the anomaly was rectified. So it was in this year that the Berwick upon Tweed mayor declared the good people of Russia are now safe!

'Torpedoes' in Berwick upon Tweed

Since 1754 Gretna Green has been synonymous with weddings. Couples eloping to Scotland could take advantage of the more relaxed marriage laws over the border. Historically, couples could not marry in England under 21 years old without a parent's consent. In Scotland, the 19th century law allowed 16 year olds to marry without parental consent. The first house you see as you enter Gretna is a registry office with "First House in Scotland Marriage Room" or "Last House in Scotland" depending on which way you approach it. It is a single-storey black and white building right next to the main road. Although there are more romantic wedding venues, it does have a certain charm. Scottish law allowed that if a declaration was made before two witnesses, anybody had the authority to conduct a marriage ceremony. Gretna Green was the first easily accessible village over the Scottish border – it became a magnet for runaway couples to get married. This led to blacksmiths in Gretna (in the town centre or the green) becoming "anvil" priests as they and their families would act as witnesses and marry couples for a small fee. In spite of the change in regulations, it is still the wedding capital of Europe with 5,000 weddings per year as couples are swept away with the romance of its history. Unfortunately, wedding planners have moved in to provide themed weddings such as Elvis and Game of Thrones. After a Channel Four documentary showing Elvis Presley on a truck driving through the streets it became known as "Gretna Green – the romantic heart of the world" (See chapter three for a border crossing race from Gretna to Carlisle).

Further south in Britain, I was barely 16 years old drinking in an old pub in the centre of Liverpool near Lime Street station. Four school friends entered the pub, but it was Les who ordered the drinks as he was the one who looked over 18 years old (you did not need documentary evidence, like a passport, in those days). My dad used to give me sound advice before I went out into Liverpool "Don't mind you drinking, son, but make sure you don't get caught". We sat in the darkest corner of the pub, trying to be inconspicuous, when the police entered the dimly lit public house. I assumed that this was going to be the start of my criminal record as the police searched the pub in detail; fortunately, they were not looking for under aged drinkers but for bombs. This was the height of the troubles in Ireland which had spilled over into mainland Britain with bomb explosions in places like Birmingham, Guildford and Warrington. Liverpool, with its port lying east across the Irish Sea, was thought to be a prime target especially with the direct ferry link from Dún Laoghaire, near Dublin (not pronounced *'DoneLegHigher'* as I first thought, but Dunleary). Unfortunately, at the time of the mid 1970s, paranoia was prevalent in both Ireland and the United Kingdom. One of the reasons for the troubles was the border between Northern and Southern Ireland.

There are 208 border crossings between Northern Ireland and the Republic of Ireland. More crossings than there are between the European Union and the countries to its east which add up to only 137 (Hutton 2018). The troubled border, in the north-east of the island of Ireland, runs along the middle of 11 roads, meets in the middle of at least three bridges and dissects two ferry crossings. Its demarcation has been the scene of shifting priorities and influences, from a militarised zone to an invisible but unmistakable border (Anthony 2019). There was a solemn occasion and "real hairy" moment to quote James Joyce. Upstairs in the Duke of Wellington Hotel, Ireland was being torn into two by traitors according to the IRA. Several high-ranking, grim faced Boundary Commissioners from both sides of Ireland faced each other across a large map of Ireland. Across the map, running from right to left, was a thick red pencil line that ended just before the Atlantic Ocean – the proposed new border. In its way lay Puckoon (although it is a fictional place that Spike Milligan wrote about in his novel of the same name, it gives a sound insight into the problem). The arguments that the Boundary Commission had outlined in his Spike Milligan's book were similar to sticking pins in maps; not unlike the situation in India in which Mr Radcliffe unintentionally found himself (see Division of India chapter four). Originally intended as an internal boundary within the United Kingdom of Great Britain and Ireland, the border was created in 1921 under the United Kingdom Parliament's Government of Ireland Act of 1920. Six of the thirty-two counties of Ireland were assigned to Northern Ireland, and the rest of Ireland, comprising 26 counties, to Southern Ireland or Eire. The new border created under the Boundary Commission was extremely irregular and 499 kilometres (310 miles) in length. As a remnant of 17th century county limits, it should have followed the physical boundaries such as rivers and mountains.

The remnants of Ireland's troubled history can still be seen on its maps like the 208 road border crossings. Some roads cross the border two or three times. The situation is not helped by the different road numbering system in the two countries; British A roads became Irish N (national) roads. So the road N54/A3 crossed the border four times even though it was a stretch of road 10 kilometres (6 miles) long. Before its closure in 1957, a section of one railway line between Clones, County Monaghan and Cavan crossed the border six times in eight miles, initially with customs checks at each crossing!

Every classic pub quiz must refer to the fact that the island of Ireland's most northerly point is Malin Head, in county Donegal....yes in southern Ireland (Eire). Also, the province known as Ulster should not be attached to the UK because it is the name of one of the island's four provinces. The state of this border is certainly a tale of confusion! Communities were angry and split as roads and lanes were blocked off and removed from the map (Bonnett 2014).

Not surprisingly, the new frontier had spawned many real-life complaints. I have chosen three fictional examples, all from the book *Puckoon* (Milligan 1973) which illustrate metaphorically how tough the new boundary made it for local communities. There was a report of an accident near the river Puckoon on the Ballyshag Bridge which had been divided in two by the boundary commission. A motor car with a driver and a coach of pensioners were in collision. The car finished on the Ulster side of the border and the coach on the Republican side. As a result, the case was being heard in two countries at once. Witnesses were rushed from court to court in order to give evidence. The driver of the coach had been thrown from his seat with his body lying across the border. Unfortunately, his legs were being sued by the passengers of the coach and his top half was claiming damages from the car driver. Solicitors predicted that the case would last at least three years because of the travel involved.

The boundary commission was responsible for some ridiculous outcomes from the drawing of the red pencil line across the map. A publican in fictional Puckoon was deeply affected because he realised that most of his pub was on the south side of the border, except for two square feet in the far corner of the public bar which was on the north side. The two square feet was in Ulster where the price of drinks is 30% cheaper so every night the pub is empty apart from a crowd of skinflints huddled in that corner like Scrooges (Milligan 1973)! Sometimes the fiction is based on the reality.

In the book a funeral approached the new Border Customs Post where a guard went through the necessary formalities and showed a Customs card to the priest who was leading the funeral procession. Nothing to declare came the response. The guard asked the incredulous question about what was inside the coffin. The body of a 98-year old, recently deceased male came the reply. The border runs between the church and the graveyard, and the border guards would not let a funeral procession through unless everyone in it has a valid passport *including the deceased*. This leads to a scene in which three of the villagers take the corpse to a photographer to get their passport photos while trying to avoid letting on that he is dead (Milligan 1973).

In Northern Ireland's capital, Belfast, its barriers destroy any logical movement across the city. The wall in the notorious Crumlin Road area, built to withstand a tank attack, consisted of two and half metres high brick and reinforced steel; the concrete was one metre in thickness. Possibly built to last 1000 years, the barrier is now obsolete as it no longer separates Protestants and Catholics. The movement called "Draw Down the Walls" wanted to remove the barriers but it was an expensive task and the barriers have become tourist attractions in their own right. Although the area is not as dangerous as it used to be, tourists still need to take care when visiting. An Indian person was walking down Crumlin Road when he was accosted by local youths. They asked him where he was from and he told them the truth, India. They asked him if he was a Catholic or Protestant. The Indian explained that he was a Hindu. The youths replied by asking whether he was a Catholic Hindu or a Protestant Hindu?

Outside the city walls of Derry lies the unfortunately named neighbourhood of Bogside. The large-gable wall murals by the Bogside Artists Free Derry Corner and the Gasyard Feile Lan (the annual music and arts festival held in a former gas yard) are popular tourist attractions. The Bogside is a majority Catholic/Irish republican area and shares a border with the Protestant/Ulster loyalist enclave (see chapter five) of the

Fountain area (called Waterside on the east bank of the river Foyle).

Belfast Peace Wall (Wikimedia)

Up to 1998's Good Friday Agreement, the barriers hardened into walls just as fear had hardened into hate. The walls did not protect against the militants who hurled pipe bombs, nail bombs and coffee-can bombs over the top of the barriers. They were so high that the attackers were unlikely to know how much damage they had done on the other side, until they looked in the next day's newspaper. The government had extended many walls upward with wire mesh panels, almost growing like a living thing (Di Cintio 2016). The thirteen miles-long mix of walls, fences and barricades are known, ironically, as Peace Lines. Many of these walls have been improved with murals and even ironic "trompe l'oeils" of painted 3D streets receding into the distance. Others have been institutionalised as fence-topped brick walls and planted with tumbling shrubs and flowers. Bizarrely, none of the barriers appear on a map, in spite of the detrimental effect on any pedestrian, cyclist or driver who is forced to make a long detour (Bonnett 2014).

As a result, many of the streets are shown as continuous on a map, but satellite imagery tells a different story (see chapter four on map errors).

The future is uncertain, although it is likely that Northern Ireland will remain part of the UK and therefore the border will continue. The barricades and walls here will long outlast the barriers between the two Germanys and the two Vietnams. The political shape of a border will depend on a number of factors in the future many of which, even the comedian Spike Milligan would struggle to predict (See chapter eight for the future of borders).

CHAPTER 2
ARBITRARY AND ABSURD BORDERS

A no man's land can have several meanings: land between a border, land that may not be recognised, unclaimed land, or land that the planners did not use. If you find yourself in this uncertain land it can be even more terrifying than crossing a border.

A group of tourists hired a 4x4 to drive along a rough road through the Sani Pass, the third steepest mountain pass in the world, seeking the highest pub in Africa. It is not surprising that only 4x4s are allowed, according to the 1987 law, as there are no crash barriers on this winding road. The road is so rough locals call it 'an African massage'. The bends have names like devil's corner and suicide bend, which speak for themselves. The group travelled from South Africa towards the mountainous kingdom of Lesotho - the average height of the country is 2,500 metres above sea level. In fact, Lesotho holds the record as being the only country that lies entirely at a minimum of a thousand metres in elevation. The summit of Sani Pass, however, is almost 400 metres above the average height at 2,875 metres high. After passing through the border control of South Africa you travel 5.6 kilometres to the Lesotho border control office. So, this large and beautiful area of the Drakensberg Mountains which was placed onto the UNESCO World Heritage Site list in the year 2000 can well and truly be classed as a no man's land. By the way, apparently the highest pub in Africa, the Sani Mountain Lodge does local *Maluti* beer for 40 rand (less than £2) so well worth the visit, except for the perilous drive back down the mountainside to South Africa!

Lesotho shares the distinction of being one of only three countries in the world to be completely surrounded by another country (it is an enclave, see chapter five). The others are the Vatican (City State) and San Marino: peculiarly both are surrounded by Italy. San Marino is the third smallest country in Europe, after Vatican City and Monaco, and the fifth smallest country in the world. A sole survivor of Italy's once powerful city state network, this landlocked country hung on to power after the more powerful kingdoms of Genoa and Venice had collapsed. Its borders remain, somehow, secure in the knowledge that it is the world's oldest surviving sovereign state and the oldest republic dating back to AD 301. San Marino's 34,000 residents enjoy one of the highest GDP per capita in the world. As a result, it has no national debt and it is the only country in the world that has more cars than people (there is just nowhere to park them).

Another mountainous region that has a no man's land is Torugart Pass connecting Kyrgyzstan and China. From the Kyrgyz side of the border you enter what is called the "buffer zone" which is about 50 kilometres to the Kyrgyz immigration post. This area is now a national park and very few people come here except truck drivers and the occasional nomad. Passing through the buffer zone, you may overtake convoys of trucks approximately one-kilometre long carrying goods into China. Once arriving at the top of the pass, you will then go through passport control at an elevation of 3,740 metres above sea level. Not surprisingly it can be very cold here, even in summer. Paradoxically, at this altitude and in sub-zero temperatures, you can enter a duty-free store. At this point, you are in a very heavily controlled Chinese buffer zone which extends for about 150 kilometres passing through several checkpoints and, after about 5 hours, you finally enter the People's Republic of China.

Many people are interested in great facts and there are certain borders that come into the highest category. Khunjerab Pass is a high mountain pass on the northern border of Pakistan with China, at an elevation of 4,733 metres above sea level. The Khunjerab Pass is the highest border-crossing in the world and the highest point on the infamous Karakoram Highway. This is an extreme crossing, with severe weather and absence of oxygen themselves creating a barrier to visiting. Khunjerab is derived from two words of the local Wakhi language: 'Khun' means blood and 'Jerav' means spring water which possibly suggest one highly inhospitable border. By the way, few people realise that the highest point on earth is also the world's highest border: China and Nepal meet 8,848 metres above sea level, at the tip of Mount Everest. There is, of course, no official border post at this altitude, and it is rare there is a queue to cross. Although, during the peak climbing months of April and May, there can be a line of people waiting to reach the summit (Cheung 2019).

A huge storm blasted over the Bay of Bengal in 1971, as Cyclone Bhola stirred up sand, silt, stones and soil from the many rivers that enter the delta of the river Ganges. This load was deposited a few kilometres out to sea, and it grew quickly into a 3.5 kilometres-long and 3 kilometres-wide island (2.2 x 1.9 miles). The only living organisms on the island were some mangrove trees and some sporadic temporary fishermen. The island shifted in terms of its size and shape altering with the changing tides and seasons. One of the rivers responsible for its formation is the river Hariabhanga which, by coincidence, forms the border between Bangladesh and India. No surprise that both countries claimed the new island giving it the name of South Talpatti in Bangladesh and New Moore Island in India. The claims had extra significance because the Bay of Bengal has valuable oil and gas reserves and each country saw the opportunity to extend its territorial waters (and presumably to make money). India placed a sign of the map of India and deployed soldiers on the island who raised the Indian flag. A dispute over the boundary looked serious and this time the British, for once, were not to blame! Independent boundary experts were employed to resolve the disagreement using the idea of "thalweg" which is a German word used to describe boundary disputes. It refers to the line of a river's lowest and therefore middle flow. If a thalweg was to the west of the island, it meant New Moore belonged to Bangladesh; if it was to the east the island was India's territory. Just as the dispute became more and more difficult to settle, the island started to sink and in 2010 there were just a few trees evident, almost as though they were trying to escape from the water and perhaps the ownership dispute. Perhaps climate change was responsible for the swelling of the rivers that initially caused the New Moore island to develop, but rising sea levels may well have resulted in the recent demise of the island (Bonnett 2014).

Most borders are next to each other along lines on a map; however, if you travel along a road between Guinea and Senegal in West Africa, the distance between the borders is fully twenty seven kilometres (seventeen miles). Some tourist companies offer trips that include camping in this area of no man's land. Whilst travellers may relish the novelty of pitching a tent on this ground that no one owns, for locals who live and work here it can be less positive. They could have a national identity crisis asking such questions as: which leader do they vote for in national elections, Senegal's Macky Sall or Guinea's Alpha Conde? Does the local tourist trip advisor website end in .gn or .sn? Are goods paid for in the currency of the West African Franc or the Guinean Franc? Under which flag would they march into the Olympic Stadium? In the American travel writer Matt Brown's essay, *Life between two nations*, he stopped to ask a woman who was pounding leaves in this no man's land:

I asked in French (my Pular only goes so far), "Is this Guinea?"
"Yes," she answered.
Surprised that she even understood French, I posed a follow-up question. "Is this Senegal," I asked.

"Yes," came the reply.

"That's more like it," I thought. Just for final confirmation, I asked, "Is this France?"

"Yes," she said.

Wow! I had biked all the way to France! I would have never guessed that the French still live in straw-roofed huts.

I rode on a little further past the village and sat down on a nationless rock to eat a tuna sandwich and ponder my unanswered questions. Maybe these villagers can't be bothered by archaic, nonsensical national borders drawn up by greedy European leaders at the Conference of Berlin over 100 years ago. Perhaps they simply consider themselves African and are content to farm their corn and raise their cattle without needing to cling to a synthetic national identity.

These areas of no man's land can be negative areas with heightened insecurity and a sense of abandonment. The Africa Development Fund supports economic infrastructure projects across the continent. It has made "establishing juxtaposed checkpoints at the borders" of its member states a priority. The Guinea-Senegal border is perhaps one border that needs attention, especially as it may have an impact on free trade, unnecessary bureaucratic paperwork, bribery and, inevitably, corruption.

Lake Albert is the seventh largest lake in Africa. In 1864, the explorer Samuel Baker became the first European to discover the lake. He named it after the recently deceased Prince Albert, consort to Queen Victoria; she wasn't too upset to be ignored because Victoria had already had a rather glorious waterfall named after her on the border of Zambia and Zimbabwe in 1855. In the last century the Zairian (would be now Congolese) President Mobutu Sese Seko vainly, but temporarily, named the lake after himself. However, the name wasn't quite as catchy as plain old Albert. The border between the two countries, shown on a map as a dotted line, is subject to movement and consequently to many border disputes about Lake Albert (Bonnett 2014).

What do you give a country for its 100th birthday? A geophysicist called Bjorn Harsson came up with the idea of giving a mountain to Finland. He discovered an 'anomaly' while conducting a survey related to the Norwegian-Finnish border. Mount Halti, being the tallest mountain in Finland, had its highest peak in Norway which was just thirty-one metres from the border. The border was drawn as a straight line, a common practice (especially by the British in Africa and the Middle East - see chapter four) in 1734 when the treaty between Sweden and Denmark was signed. Historically, Norway was ruled by Denmark and Finland originally belonged to Sweden. Ever since his discovery, Harsson has been trying to convince the Norwegian government to rectify this border, so that the peak lay on the Finnish side. Harsson thought that Finland's forthcoming hundred-year independence anniversary in December 2017 would be the perfect occasion for Norway to give Mount Halti to its neighbour as a token of friendship and goodwill. The campaign involved social media with a "battle for birthday mountain" slogan. Unfortunately, there were practical problems as mountains are difficult features to move! Even harder bureaucratically it seems. Borders may look arbitrary on a map and to migratory reindeers, but to people and their governments any change to borders has major political and legal consequences.

Spices today are commonplace in supermarkets and relatively inexpensive and packaged in glass jars, in vacuum packs or even sold in frozen packages. The desire to dominate the trade of spices in the past has been the aim of several countries especially Portugal, Spain, the Netherlands and England. The Spice Islands (known as the Moluccas) are a small group of islands to the north-east of Indonesia, between Celebes and New Guinea. They include Halmahera (the largest), Seram, Ambon, Ternate and the Aru and Kai island groups. They were known for being the largest producers of mace, nutmeg, cloves and pepper in the world. Spices had been available in Europe throughout the Middle Ages, but the prices were very high mainly because they had to be shipped expensively overland and through the hands of many traders. Each trader made a profit and by the time the spices arrived in Venice (the chief point of trade and contact between Europe and the East) they were often worth 1000% more than the original price paid for them in the Spice Islands. The Portuguese began buying spices directly from the Spice Islands as early as the 1520s but were not pleased when the Spanish brought back spices from the islands to threaten the Portuguese monopoly. In order to argue their case, the Portuguese cited the infamous Treaty of Tordesillas signed in 1494. In the treaty, Pope Alexander VI had drawn a line down the middle of the Atlantic Ocean from pole to pole some hundred leagues west of the Cape Verde islands. Any land discovered west of this line belonged to Spain. Every landmass found east of the line, declared the Pope, belonged to Portugal. Rather cleverly, the Portuguese had managed to move the line westwards by hundreds of miles (with some diplomatic bargaining) allowing them to argue that Brazil, whose coastline was cut by the line, belonged to Portugal. A good piece of cartography and real-estate business as they ended up with the longest beach in the world - the 150 kilometre Praia do Cassino beach in Brazil! The Pontiff's line was easy to administer close to Europe but as many maps were inaccurate in the sixteenth century, there was a dispute over the sovereignty of the Spice Islands in Asia. There were five years of disagreement over the ownership of the islands before King Charles V of Spain sold his claim to the Spice Islands for the huge sum of 350,000 gold ducats (about £37 million pounds today). This sale by the Spanish king solved the problem, until sixty years later Dutch and English ships started to set foot on the islands. Under the backing of Queen Elizabeth 1st, a flotilla of ships set sail for the Spice Islands under the command of Sir Francis Drake. The British claimed the island of Run in Indonesia which at three kilometres long and one kilometre wide was one of the smallest of the Banda Islands. Amazingly, it was the only place in the world, at the time, that grew nutmeg and mace (which surprisingly came from the same tree): nutmeg is from the seed and mace is from the seed covering. The Spice Islands remained so desirable, prestigious and exotic that when King James I gained possession of two small islets, it was such a coup that for a time he was pleased to style himself "King of England, Scotland, Ireland, France, Puloway and Puloroon" (Bryson 2010). The island of Run was officially given to the Dutch in 1664 but in return the British gained the island of Manhattan and New York (formerly New Amsterdam). Under current real estate prices such as over $2000 per square foot in 2021, this can only be classed as an extremely smart piece of estate management! (Milton 1999) Indonesia has 16,000 islands and over 735,000 square miles of sea so it is little wonder that the locations of the Moluccas or Spice Islands remained a mystery to Europeans for so long.

Perhaps some of the biggest disagreements over borders is not the argument over countries, but that concerning continents. Sport can play an enormous part to improve cross border/country relationships. Running is a feature of crossing borders, and horse racing, volleyball and even cricket can have positive impacts (see chapter three). So, not to exclude the popular game of football, the European Football Championships have as their motto "football without frontiers". However, it would have been amazing if a team from behind the "iron curtain" could have won the championships at some stage. But, what if Israel, which is not in Europe but in the Middle East, had won the European football championships? Israel has not only competed in the UEFA football Championships, but also competed in other European competitions, such as European athletics and the Eurovision Song Contest (winning it four times in 1978, 1979, 1999 and as recently as 2018). What if Australia had won the Eurovision song contest? Perhaps the history of the boundaries of continents need closer inspection.

To a geographer, the boundaries between the continents on earth are generally a matter of geographical convention. The modern atlas that was bought last week should be up to date and accurate, although unfortunately it is not necessarily correct! For example, the modern border between Asia and Europe remains a historical and cultural construct, defined only by convention. The modern border follows the Aegean Sea, the Dardanelles–Sea of

Marmara–Bosphorus (together known as the Turkish Straits), the Black Sea, along the watershed of the Greater Caucasus, the north western portion of the Caspian Sea and along the Ural River and Ural Mountains to the Kara Sea (Wikipedia: "Boundaries between continents of the earth"). These locations are mapped and listed in most atlases including that of the National Geographic Society and as described in the World Factbook (a reference resource produced by the CIA!). This boundary between Europe and Asia is unusual among continental boundaries because of its largely mountain and river based characteristics north and east of the Black Sea. The reason is historical, because the division of Europe and Asia goes back to the early Greek geographers. In the modern sense of the term "continent", Eurasia is more readily identifiable as a "continent", and Europe has occasionally been described as a subcontinent of Eurasia. The nature of this boundary means that some countries are in both continents such as Russia, Turkey, Kazakhstan, Azerbaijan, Georgia and Armenia (just to confuse geography scholars).

Recently I was asked how many countries are in Europe. An easy question but with a somewhat complex answer. There are 51 independent states but only 49 if you exclude Cyprus and Armenia which are geographically in Asia, but politically in Europe. 53 if you include Transnistria (part of Moldova), and South Ossetia (part of Georgia). These are disputed territories but recognised by some countries. 46 is the answer if the question was which countries are completely in Europe because you would exclude Turkey, Russia, Kazakhstan, Azerbaijan, Georgia. There are only 44 recognised by the United Nations (sovereign states or nations). 52 if you include "The Sovereign Order of Malta" which is a sovereign entity. It has no territory as such but some regard it as the smallest sovereign state in the world. You can get the number up to over 60 if you add in self-proclaimed republics in Europe or micronations such as Liberland (Croatia/Serbia), Sealand (off the UK coast), Christiania (Denmark), Vukovar (Serbia/Croatia), Ladonia (Sweden), Tavolara (island off the coast of Sardinia),

Saugeais (France), Kugelmugel (Austria) and Elleore (Denmark) (see chapter seven).

I believe that there is something about intercontinental (meaning between two or more continents) countries that make them quirky. For example, Armenia, the country where chess is a compulsory subject in school. Chess is part of the primary school curriculum and valued as much as maths and history. It is a national obsession, so if you visit and challenge the local school children to a game, don't expect an easy win! Many Armenians are still convinced Noah's Ark is embedded in ice atop the impressive Mount Ararat. Just as proof, a piece of the Ark can even be viewed in Armenia's Etchmiadzin Cathedral Museum. In another intercontinental country, Kazakhstan, the most popular dish is called Kazy and is a smoked horsemeat sausage. The country's most popular sport, "Buzkashi", which literally means "grabbing the dead goat", sees players on horseback vie for control of the "ball", which, as the name suggests, is the headless carcass of a goat. After a game, the players all have a party where players drink the national drink which is made from fermented horse milk (not urine as Borat would have you believe in the 2006 film).

The usual line taken to divide Africa from Asia today is at the Isthmus of Suez, the narrowest gap between the Mediterranean and Gulf of Suez, which is the route today followed by the Suez Canal. This makes the Sinai Peninsula geographically Asian, and Egypt an intercontinental country. Less than 2% of the Egyptian population live in the Sinai, and hence Egypt, even though technically transcontinental, is usually considered an African country entirely and not partly Asian. To complicate matters, Egypt is also included in the Middle East which, of course, is classed as Asia.

Europe and North America are separated by the North Atlantic Ocean. In terms of associating its oceanic islands with either continent, the boundary is usually drawn between Greenland and Iceland, and between Bermuda and the Azores. Iceland and the Azores are protrusions of the Mid-Atlantic Ridge and are associated with and populated by people from Europe, even though they are areas that are on the North American Plate.

The Bering Strait and Bering Sea separate the landmasses of Asia and North America, as well as forming the important international boundary between the countries of Russia and the United States. This national and continental boundary separates the Diomede Islands in the Bering Strait, with Big Diomede in Russia and Little Diomede in the U.S.A. (see chapter six).

Many people believe that there could have been more creativity in naming North America, Central America, South America and the United States of America (see chapter six for information on Columbus). The border between North America and South America is at some point on the Isthmus of Panama. The most common demarcation in atlases and other sources follows the Darién Mountains watershed that divides along the Colombia–Panama border where the Isthmus meets the South American continent. Virtually all atlases list Panama as a state falling entirely within North America, but atlases are not always correct.

You can tell an Australian abroad if they are wearing thongs, shorts and have a beer in their hand at ten o'clock in the morning (see chapter eight - avoiding stereotypes). Australia is the country that is the home to many animals that, to put it simply, can kill you. However, it is also a continent as well. To avoid any obvious confusion, Oceania is sometimes used to describe the continent. In the geopolitical framework used by the United Nations, by the International Olympic Committee, and by many atlases, Oceania includes Australia and the nations of the Pacific from Papua New Guinea east, but not Indonesian New Guinea. In order to help to simplify the situation, it is Australasia, Melanesia, Micronesia and Polynesia. To the north, its boundary can be divided by a variety of lines - the Wallace line or Lyddeker line or Weber line. Wallace's Line is a faunal boundary line drawn in 1859 by the British naturalist Alfred Russel Wallace. This line is a hypothetical line separating Asia (west) and Australasia's (east) marsupial animals. In 1895, Lydekker's Line (Richard Lydekker was a British natural historian) delineated the biogeographical boundary through Indonesia that separates Wallacea to the west from Australia-New Guinea to the east. The Weber line, which was pioneered by Max Weber who was a German-Dutch zoologist and bio-geographer, is an imaginary line separating flora and fauna north of Australia. Many people struggle with the location of the boundary of Asia and Australasia because of the three different lines. However, with the three lines to choose from, perhaps it should be easy, compared to some other continental boundaries of the world.

Inevitably, there are some countries that are represented in more than one continent rather than just spanning two continents. France (in Europe) is represented in all continents apart from Asia! Examples are Guadeloupe in North America, French Guiana in South America, Reunion in Africa, French Polynesia in Oceania, and Adelie Land in Antarctica. It is no wonder that the French Foreign Legion is kept so busy! The United Kingdom has overseas territories on five continents: North America (the Bermuda Islands), Europe (Gibraltar and the British Isles not including Ireland), South America (the Falkland Islands), Antarctica (British Antarctic Territory) and Asia (British Indian Ocean Territory). The only overseas territory that is in just three continents (rather than France and UK, which have more than three) is the European Kingdom of the Netherlands: Aruba, Bonaire and Curacao are just off the coast of Venezuela and would count as South America, while St Martin, St Eustatius and Saba are further north and considered to be located in North America.

You would think that the borders of continents would be easy to define, but as outlined in this chapter, they can be very complicated. Crossing borders may be even more elaborate…

CHAPTER 3
COOL BORDER CROSSINGS /
RUNNING ACROSS BORDERS

There is a place that is a border enthusiast's nirvana, where you can enjoy a beer or white wine in a bar whilst straddling the line of Europe's wonkiest border. The small town of Baarle dissects the two countries of Belgium and the Netherlands despite being five kilometres on the Dutch side of the border. Within and around the town there are fully twenty-one separate exclaves (see chapter five) of Belgium which contain five further enclaves of the Netherlands; the smallest is only two-thirds of an acre. Of the world's 260 enclaves about 12% exist in and around Baarle. It arises from a succession of treaties over a thousand years between the Lords of Breda and the Dukes of Brabant. Visitors can easily distinguish the borders as both town councils have marked them with crosses on the road and pavements, conveniently painting either side with B or NL. Tourists have photograph opportunities with a foot either side of the divide, similar to straddling the Greenwich meridian in London, or in my case a drink either side of the crosses in a bar (see illustration). I am not quite sure what would happen during the interesting scenario of when the Dutch play Belgium in the European football championships! Where would the residents choose to watch the match in a bar with a television screen? Would they cross the border to be with fellow supporters?

Despite the signage, it is not always clear which country you are in and it is possible to walk in a straight line across five national borders in one minute. Dutch and Belgium royalty and politicians use the town for mutual accords to be signed in the Enclave Room in the Den Engel Hotel (The Angel Hotel). Officially it is two towns: Baarle-Hertog (population 2,306) in Belgium, and Baarle-Nassau (population 6,668) in the Netherlands. Here, there are two of everything such as town halls, fire departments, phone companies, websites (.be and .nl), languages (Flemish and Dutch) and police chief constables who sit in the same public building. Unbelievably, some houses have their front door in one country and their back door in another. In Baarle, the local law is that tax is paid to the country where one's front door is. As a result, some residents have changed their back doors to the front to take advantage of better tax arrangements. The number plaques identify the nationality of a house – red, white and blue for Dutch; black, gold and red for Belgium. To identify which side of the line a deceased person originated from, even the cemetery is demarcated with small metal country flags (presumably of the same colours). The gentle and wealthy farming flatlands of the two countries belie the tension of the past but farmers enjoy the prosperity of the present as tourist coaches swell the town's car parks and the profits of the local shops.

Bar in Baarle-Hertog (Wikimedia)

Historically, most enclaves in this area had been re-integrated into Napoleonic France. It was the Treaty of Maastricht in 1843 (not the EU's 1992 version!) signed in the Netherlands near the border with Germany that delimited the boundary between the Netherlands and Belgium. After the signing, it was still found to be impossible to compromise on the territory of Baarle. Instead of defining a boundary, it was accepted that the nationality of over 5,000 parcels of land be established, one by one, which gave a great opportunity for geographers to complete their favourite pastime - the colouring of maps!

As if the town of Baarle-Hertog is not interesting enough, there is a cafe here staffed mainly by Down's syndrome trainees named "Brownies & downieS" which apparently sells good coffee (www.Browniesanddowniesleeuwarden.nl). The tax on coffee is higher in Belgium than Holland, but the cafe cannot raise their coffee prices because customers might just go to a neighbouring café across the border. Dutch businesses that help people with disabilities get support from the government, but Belgian businesses do not so it may have made more sense to have set up the cafe a little further down the street. One senses that the borders here are more difficult to alter as they are more than just a geographic border: they have become almost a way of life. The towns have even bid to be listed as a UNESCO World Heritage Site, for their unique cross-border co-operation.

There still is hope for border conformists (countries that comply with border standards and rules) in this part of the world. As an example of border restructuring, the Netherlands and Belgium agreed a land swap equivalent of around twenty-seven football pitches, to make the border run through the middle of the River Meuse (Belgium spelling) or Maas (to give it the Dutch spelling). Belgium agreed to swap territory and give more land than it receives. The reason for this change comes down to people straightening the river. After Belgium gained independence from the Netherlands in 1830, the border was drawn on maps along the Meuse. However, in 1961, the river was straightened to make navigation easier, placing parts of each country's territory on the other side of the river. With the border as it was, the only way to reach land without crossing into another country was by boat (Reuters 2016). By swapping territory, common sense has prevailed which is highly unusual for a border area.

In another river border continent or region, the Yalu river in front of Hyenseo Lee's house was just eleven yards wide and relatively shallow. In her book *The Girl with Seven Names* she describes how this river became a heavily guarded border between North Korea and China. Any human activity would invite suspicion as the border guards closely watched the women who climbed down the bank to fetch water and wash clothes. They were watching in case the women were receiving contraband or waiting for a moment to cross the river border illegally. The river acted as a prison fence although eventually the women paid off the North Korean guards so that they could cross. Hyenseo Lee describes how she waded waist-deep through the water with her mother and brother to China even though there were nine, armed, border guards in the area (Lee 2015).

The Military Demarcation Line (MDL), sometimes referred to as the Armistice Line, is the land border between North Korea and South Korea. On either side of the line is no man's land called the Korean Demilitarized Zone (DMZ). The MDL and DMZ were established by the Armistice at the end of the Korean War in 1953. In the Korean language, the line means armistice line or possibly refers to the "38th parallel" which is a name that was used at the end of World War II, when Japan was defeated in 1945. It was an arbitrary decision to use this line of latitude made in the White House on a basic National Geographic map, without the presence of Koreans or Americans with Korean expertise! The line on the ground is marked off by a series of 1,292 identical signs which are placed at intervals across the peninsula. The north facing side of the signs are written in Korean and Chinese, and on the south facing side they are written in Korean and English. The signs are now ageing and rusting away; one hopes that this old border line will be removed soon.

North Korea has an army of over a million soldiers which is staggering as it only has a population of 23 million, and 70% of those soldiers can be deployed quickly to reach the border within 12 hours. You may have imagined that the capital of South Korea is well away from the potential flashpoint of the DMZ; however, Seoul is only 35 miles away: well within easy reach of North Korean missiles or even an invasion from an army. In spite of politically charged threats, actual confrontations occur almost entirely within the half-mile wide enclave of Panmunjom, the DMZ's "truce village" where the opposing sides come to talk. Here, the most notorious incident occurred in 1976 when North Korean troops, upset at a tree-cutting operation near one of their guard towers, clubbed two American officers to death with axe handles. Panmunjom is little more than a collection of no-frills conference rooms bisected by the MDL. It is the one place where delegates from North Korea and the UN meet to discuss military, political and logistical matters. You might think this is a grown-up type of place, but the UN Command force describe it as "like a schoolyard with two bullies poking each other in the eye (National Geographic 2003).

North and South Korea border (Wikimedia)

Tourists enter North Korea or the Democratic People's Republic of Korea ('democratic' is a misnomer if ever there was one) through China and you must have an expensive guide at all times or be on a guided tour (slightly less expensive). It is recommended that you call the country DPRK rather than North Korea because, according to the Kim dynasty, North Korea is the only Korea. It is the centre and not north of anything (try explaining that to a geography GCSE class). You would imagine that the border guards on the train from China into DPRK are thorough and ruthless. In fact, in the most paranoid, security conscious country in the world, bags need not be opened, and phones are left alone. Laptops are a different matter but difficult to check on a train. The technology DPRK experts look for one item in particular: an American 2014 film, ranked poorly with only 48% approval on the Rotten Tomatoes website, called "The Interview" starring Seth Rogan and James Franco. It dramatises the execution of Kim Jong-un and so incensed the regime that, allegedly, they hacked into the Sony organisation and released many personal embarrassing details of employees as revenge. Many people believe that this incident reinforces the notion that the regime lacks any sort of sense of humour (Fletcher 2018). When *Monty Python* star Michael Palin visited North Korea, the airport was pristine and remained that way because there were no other passengers. The ghostly international airport, in the newly built beachside resort town of Wonsan, was opened by leader Kim Jong-un who gave the farcical order that arrival and departure passengers should be kept apart. What a remarkably good idea! His knowledge of transport knows no depths. Although this may be obvious guidance, the lack of other passengers, apart from Palin and his film crew, made it risible. Michael Palin, annoyed officials during this first day of filming the Channel 5 documentary *Michael Palin in North Korea* when his hands (in his pockets) became obscured as he spoke to the camera in front of two statues of the country's former leaders. If you have your hands in your pockets, it can be seen as disrespectful to the Kim family, so some scenes had to be re-shot (Palin 2019).

The geography of the continent of Europe is dominated by a series of natural features such as mountains, rivers and valleys. In part, it explains why it has developed over centuries into fairly small countries. An example is France that is bordered by natural barriers such as the Alps, Pyrenees, Rhine, the Atlantic Ocean and the Mediterranean Sea. Europe's major rivers have a tendency not to meet so it means they can act as boundaries. It partly explains why there are so many European countries in a relatively small space. Each European river has its own economic sphere of influence expanding into an urban area, which may also explain why the capitals tend to be on major riverbanks. A cruise along the river Danube, the continent's second longest river at 1,780 miles long (2865 kilometres), can further explain Europe's borders. From its source in Germany, the Danube's basin affects eighteen countries forming natural borders along its course. It established the border of the Roman Empire over 2,000 years ago creating one of the great medieval trading routes. The river Danube also formed the borders of two more recent empires: the Austro-Hungarian and the Ottoman.

Because the Danube is difficult to navigate, it is perhaps not the ideal river to travel along, especially in a small sailing craft. However, AJ Mackinnon (Sandy), on his unlikely voyage along the Danube, sailed in a mirror dinghy called "Jack de Crow" (named after a jackdaw nesting at Ellesmere school, Shropshire where he was teaching) with cheerful optimism and wearing a pith helmet. His hilarious, if eccentric, journey in the boat took him from North Wales to the Black Sea, covering 4,900 miles (7,886 kilometres) under sail, oar and occasionally tow rope via more than 280 locks. One of his excellent stories begins when AJ reaches Kelheim on the Danube (German name Donau) and sees a Parthenon (no, not the one in Athens), a gleaming temple in which the marble, with every pillar and cornice intact, looked like it had been completed last week. In fact, this Parthenon was an exact full-scale copy of the original Parthenon in Greece. It had been commissioned by King Ludwig the Sane the 1st (you can guess what the second one was called) in 1807, the man who had also built the important Rhine-Main-Donau Canal. The Valhalla, as it is called, is a hall of fame that honours distinguished people throughout German history with sculptures represented as busts; examples are Einstein and Brahms. It was given the name Valhalla (German Walhalla), which is a Norse word (in Norse mythology a majestic and huge hall ruled over by the god Odin), and as AJ Mackinnon suggests if there was ever an edifice that is less Norse, it would be difficult to conceive (Mackinnon 2002).

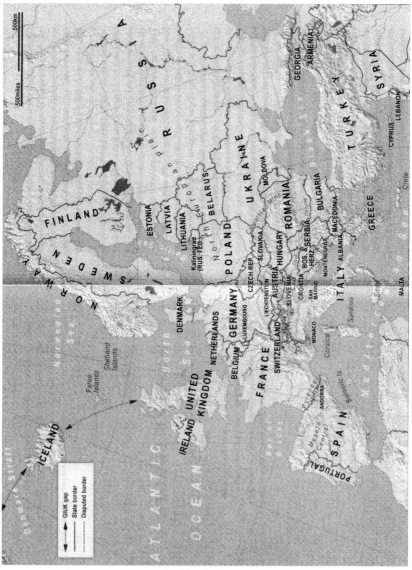

Illustration of a map of Europe (JP Map graphics Ltd)

Montenegro is famous for border crossings in both the north and south of the country. Staying near Dubrovnik in Croatia I thought a day trip to Montenegro looked appealing so a hire car was booked, with a warning from the car hire company of major traffic delays at the border. To confuse money matters, Croatia which is in the EU uses its own currency the kuna; Montenegro which is not in the EU uses the euro (some things are just not logical). About 6 miles from the start of our journey, we arrived at the border with a two-hour queue of vehicles. When we approached the border guards, they saw the EU passport colour and waved us through in a matter of seconds. Montenegro's inland Bay of Kotor and the coastline at Budva were explored in a day and the border was re-visited to return to the blue waters around Dubrovnik. This time the return border crossing involved a four hour wait to get back into Croatia because this was the most southerly entry point into the EU and so an important crossing. If people could get across here, virtually all of Europe was accessible (see Schengen agreement chapter one). There were some stray but friendly dogs who walked along the road alongside our car as we gently edged our way to the border post. The dogs walked through the border patrol quickly and without a hitch, unlike the cars with the identification marks "AL" (Albania) that went through a detailed search by security guards. Mike Parker in his book *Map Addict* was fearful of this southern crossing from Montenegro to Albania. Podgorica (formerly Titograd) is only fifteen miles (twenty-four kilometres) from the border. Although there is a railway line no trains use it and there are no buses. The only way is to find a taxi to the frontier is to walk through the border and then hope there is someone on the other side who could extend the journey. His border crossing was going smoothly until the guard saw the UK passport; he stood up and broke into a grin saying "Anglia! Meester Bean, Norman Wisdom, Tony Blair". Mike Parker was embarrassed to be associated with a country that was famous for "three gurning clowns". In spite of a weak Norman Wisdom impression by Mike, he walked into what used to be called "Europe's last Stalinist state" where, by a miracle of capitalism, a taxi appeared on the Albanian road so he could continue his journey (Parker 2010).

You would expect to find Europe's second longest railway platform (a staggering 200 metres long) probably to be in one of Europe's largest metropolises such as Paris or Rome: in fact it is in a mountainside village called Canfranc that has a population of just over 500 people. The railway at Canfranc was expected to be a link between two nations involving much tunnelling of hard rock in order to open up travel between France and Spain. Canfranc railway station stood high up in the Pyrenees, on the Spanish side of the border, characterised by late art nouveau architecture. This grand station's opening was in 1928 attended by the French President Gaston Doumergue and the Spanish King Alfonso XlII. The main station building boasted 365 windows apparently representing one for each day of the year (clearly ignoring the fact that 1928 was a leap year!). Any cross-border travellers were forced to change trains here owing to the different rail gauges between France and Spain. In 1929, due to the Wall Street crash, passenger demand sank to less than fifty per day, giving the station its nickname "The Titanic of the mountains". It has an ignominious past: closed down by Franco during the Spanish Civil War; served as an escape route for Jews fleeing fascism; and as a means of communication for Allied spies in the Second World War. Since the local government in Aragon purchased the station, encouragingly rail travel through the Pyrenees has started up again, even though there are still only two local trains a day running on its tracks (Elborough 2018).

Crossing the border from Spain to Portugal can take many different forms such as the car, train or a sedate boat trip if there is a river to cross. However, one of the most exhilarating ways is the border crossing over the River Guadiana from Spain to Portugal on the first cross-border zip wire line. Along the 720 metres joining the two countries you can skim over the river at speeds between 70 and 80 kilometres per hour. You could argue that you are time travelling because you literally fly through time and gain one hour because of the time zone difference between the two countries. The "Limite Zero" zip wire journey lasts 60 seconds and connects Sanlúcar de Guadiana in Spain to Alcoutim in Portugal. It is a thrill-seekers opportunity to tackle the only cross-border zip wire challenge in the world, and test if you have symptoms of vertigo!

Crossing borders in Russia, the largest country in the world, is on a different scale altogether. Here, environmentalists have tracked eagles by attaching a device that automatically texts its location and exact position to a control centre. Unfortunately, the Russian eagle was able to fly longer distances than first thought, for example from Kazakhstan and all the way to Iran. It built up a staggeringly large bill of roaming and text charges as it flew oblivious to the cost of the bills from various mobile phone companies.

The author John Mole travelled to Russia to try to sell to the Russians, of all things, the concept of British baked potato restaurants. He tells an amusing story:

"I went into a church in Moscow where a service was going on with a lovely choir. It was packed except for a side chapel. This may have been because the main occupants were two dead old ladies, lying in open coffins. One of them had lots of mourners congregating around her, surrounded by flowers and candles. The other woman had nothing and nobody. I felt sorry for her on her own, so I lit a candle and stuck it on her coffin. When I backed off another little old lady grabbed my arm. I got a shock because she looked just like the dead one. 'She knew you'd come' she said. She dragged me off to an old man leaning on two sticks. I was scared in case it was my putative father. But she stuck his hand in mine and told me to take him outside to the soup kitchen next door. He was a horrible yellow colour and covered in bright red scabs and had the worst case of the shakes. We shimmied and shook down the aisle and when we got outside he steered us to a whitewashed shack that was a makeshift lavatory. He had a lot of trouble undoing himself and he said 'hold it please'. Lord, in for a penny…I took it out for him. Remarkably, and very conveniently, it was the only bit of him that didn't shake. I tried to think beautiful thoughts as he looked up at me and said 'I only wanted you to hold my stick, but thanks anyway."

Russian humour is not particularly well known in the western world. I remember thinking that the first time I saw Mikhail Gorbachev, the eighth leader of the Soviet Union, on television, his famous facial birthmark looked just like a map of Thailand. However, I very much doubt that the Thai people were ever on his mind!

The same border, of course, can be guarded in different ways by neighbouring countries. On the Greek side of the Greek/Turkish border, for instance, officials can wave you through with yawns and an easy-going attitude. However, on the Turkish side you can be greeted by armed soldiers in camouflage uniform with MKEK sub-machine guns over their shoulders. They may decide to dismantle your car or unscrew a brass souvenir possibly looking for hashish or cocaine. It makes you sweat and think of the condition of the prisons in the film *Midnight Express.* Between Greece and Turkey is a long corridor with high walls of barbed wire, "tight and one-directional like a birthing canal" (Kassobova 2017). In the same area of Europe, Bulgarian summer package holidays are famous for good value, sand and sunshine on the shores of the Black Sea. In the 1960s the tourism industry was big business but also totalitarian because everything belonged to the State, even the sand. Apparently every second barman was in the service of the Bulgarian State Security to some extent, while a specially trained "operational group" of KGB, Czech and Stasi agents were disguised as holidaymakers (I will not suggest any jokes about what was inside their Speedos). The local Bulgarians called the East German holidaymakers "the sandals", because it was dressed in their sandals and beach clothes that they would sneak away from the beach at night in order to escape into the Bulgarian dark forest in an area called Strandja and attempt to cross the border (or granitza in Bulgarian). Those who didn't go through the forest went south to the coast towards Turkey in diving suits, on inflatable beach dinghies and on lilos, furiously paddling away, until they were swept out to sea. It was no use hoping you would float to the other side of the tide-less Black Sea because, of course, that land belonged to the oppressive Soviet Union. The red Riviera, as it was known, was a long walk to the Turkish border through Strandja's forested hills that were full of dangers of not only armed guards and but also bears. You needed an "otkrit list" to visit Strandja which was an official permit from the Ministry of Internal Affairs. Fundamentally, that meant you couldn't visit. This border or "grenzzone" was difficult to cross because it had an electrified barbed wire and guarded fence all the way along the border, although many people still attempted to escape.

The three-border town of Svilengrad (about 19,000 inhabitants) is situated in the south eastern part of Bulgaria next to the frontiers with Greece and Turkey. It lies in the Maritsa River Valley between the Sakar and the Rhodope mountains on the major transcontinental road connecting Istanbul and Asia with Vienna and Europe, just 180 kilometres away from the Aegean Sea. The three border rivers (called Arda, Tundja and Evros-Maritsa) flood almost every year - if a dam upstream in Bulgaria opened a sluice gate, both Turkey and Greece would be flooded. Indeed, this border has seen many spill-overs and upheavals over the years. One such upheaval includes the catastrophic "exchange of populations" after the Balkan Wars of 1912-13, when borders were redrawn and many in Bulgaria, Greece and Turkey found themselves in alien territory overnight (similar to other places such as Palestine in 1948 and Berlin in 1961). They had to run for their lives across the newly formed border lines. The name of the town Svilengrad means Silk Town because of the vibrant silk industry that had been developed here until the early twentieth century. Today, the major businesses in the area are the wine industry and particularly gambling (since gambling is illegal in Turkey and highly restricted in Greece, more than 10 of these Bulgarian local casinos attract gamblers from the neighbouring countries). There are casinos with pertinent names called "Pasha", "Ali Baba" and "Saray" that promised "shows, prizes and many more surprises". Greeks also come over the border for many of their essential needs, such as haircuts in Bulgaria and fake Levi jeans in Turkey. Probably no surprise that there is a lot less money in people's wallets for the return journey!

East Germany, or the German Democratic Republic (GDR), was a state that existed from 1949 to 1990, the period when the eastern portion of Germany was part of the Eastern Bloc during the Cold War. The GDR was Soviet Russia's poster girl representing a flagship western outpost where their brand of communism almost survived. No one queued for food, welfare provisions were the envy of many in the West, education standards were some of the highest in the world, and it was ranked the twelfth strongest economy in 1984 by the World Bank. After recognition by the International Olympic Committee in 1968, the GDR finished every Olympic Games from 1972 onwards in the top three of the medals table (of course, many sports journalists believe it was with the help of performance enhancing drugs). This East German border with West Germany, and the West, was part of the "Iron Curtain" (see chapter one). It was protected by over 47,000 GDR border guards who were often stationed in boring and miserable locations. It is no surprise to learn that 2,500 border guards escaped to the west. All the guards had passed an advanced marksmanship test with the ability to hit two moving targets with four shots at a range of 200 metres, both in the day or at night. One of those guards was Jurgen Lange who was a teenager on national service. He was patrolling a mountainous and lonely border stretch with his superior sergeant because, for obvious reasons, they were not allowed to guard alone. They were under strict orders to shoot to kill if a colleague tried to escape: indeed 37 guards in total were fatally gunned down by border guard colleagues whilst trying to escape. His sergeant started scaling up the border fence and, after raising his rifle, Lange decided not to shoot allowing his sergeant to escape to the West. Lange realised that by not shooting his fellow soldier he faced a long stint in prison, so he followed his superior over the fence.

When the West Germans met him on the other side, they took away his gun but realised that it wouldn't fire - the sergeant had taken the sensible precaution of disabling the gun before the pair went out on patrol (Moore 2016).

Czechoslovakia is famous for changing its borders. In 1993 it split into two countries, Slovakia and the Czech Republic, unusually by peaceful means called the Velvet Revolution or sometimes called the Gentle Revolution. According to local research, areas where Czechoslovakia had three electrified fences along the Iron Curtain wall are now avoided by a generation of deer who never encountered them in their lifetime (BBC 2014). Scientists have found that over 30 years after the Iron Curtain came down, central European deer still balk at crossing areas where there used to be electrified fences. A seven-year study in Sumava national park, in the Czech Republic, discovered that red deer, wearing GPS equipped collars, were still wary of locations where the former Czechoslovakia had three parallel electrified fences patrolled by heavily armed guards. Nearly 500 people were killed when they tried to escape the country across the frontier with Germany, and deer were killed too. It appears that deer fawns follow their mothers for the first year of their life and learn from them where to go, and where not to go!

Brothels appeared in border areas of the Czech Republic in the early 1990s, shortly after the fall of the communist regime and the opening of the country's borders. The sex market was developed here by the economic differential between the Czech Republic and its west European neighbours, especially German-speaking clientele. The trucking routes between the Czech Republic, Germany and Austria have often been described as "sex roads" or even "slave markets". Without knowledge of first-hand experience, there are, allegedly, "nightclubs" (not the sort you have in UK cities) - effectively brothels - along a 150 kilometre border between the Czech Republic and Bavaria.

Nicholas Crane halfway through his year-long walking trip from Cape Finisterre to Istanbul stopped at a small town called

Piwniczna in Poland. The town derived a living from straddling the border with Slovakia. Signs bearing the words *Uwaga! Zly pies* covered gateways throughout the town. He wondered why he was being warned of sly pies, poisonous pasties, sneaky steak puddings or killer quiches. Apparently, "pies" in Polish translates as dog so the signs were a warning about dangerous dogs (Crane 1996).

If you have ever watched a Disney film starring John Hurt called *Night Crossing* you will know about the desperate measures that people go to and plan in order to cross a border. It is the story of Herr Strelzyk who gained worldwide fame when he fled the communist dictatorship of East Germany on September 16, 1979, landing in free West Germany. This true story was also made into a dramatic German film *Ballon* in 2018. For years Herr Strelzyk and others constructed a balloon in secrecy by sewing together raincoats and other fabrics. The real-life fabric makers were on the film-set telling the director about the thickness of the material that was crucial to their escape. They had a cameo role as café customers at the end of the film. There were several previous, unsuccessful attempts and even a fire on board until the two families, Strelzyk and Wetzel, flew over the border crossing at Rudolphstein on the A9_road. When the propane in the hot air burners ran out they descended quickly, landing near the town of Naila, in the West German state of Bavaria and only 10 kilometres (6 miles) from the border with East Germany. However, they were not sure that they had made it over the border. The families looked for clues and saw modern farm equipment in the field which was very different from East German agricultural machines. Another clue was given by the police who first spotted them in the West: they were driving a stylish Audi, not a car they would have previously seen in East Germany.

In fact, East Germans were more likely to drive a Trabant 601—the most popular car in East Germany before the collapse of the Iron Curtain. Over the years, the "Trabi" (as it's affectionately known) has been the butt of endless jokes associated with East German industry. With its bare interior, oddly-designed gear lever, and an exterior made of Duroplast (a rust-resistant, cotton-reinforced resin plastic that's lighter and stronger than steel and more importantly could be manufactured in the GDR), the standard four-seater Trabi sedan has been referred to as one of the "worst cars ever built". My Fiat 127 ran it a close second when I tried to run and repair it as a student. In addition, the Trabi contained a two-stroke engine, the same kind used in lawnmowers and tuk-tuks found in Asia, so it is understandable why there are so many Trabi jokes. My favourite is "Why does a Trabi have a heated rear window? *To keep your hands warm while you push.*" The car was produced over a very long time, in fact from 1957 until 1991, earning the derogatory nicknames "spark plug with a roof" and "cardboard racer" because of its seemingly inferior design. You would think they could have got the design correct after producing it for 34 years. To many Westerners, the Trabi remains a prime example of East German repression and the governing Socialist United Party's archaic ways. Trabis had no fuel gauge, no air conditioning, no indicators or brake lights, and could only reach a maximum speed of 62 miles per hour. Although that speed would probably suffice when travelling up and down the busy M1 in 5pm rush hour in the UK. Once the Berlin Wall came down, Trabis just couldn't compete with Western vehicles such as BMW and Volkswagen, and seemingly overnight East Germany's most coveted car became almost obsolete.

East Germany had another defiantly Spartan workhorse - not a car this time but a bicycle. Not just any cycle but a folding cycle called a MIFA an acronym for Mitteldeutsche Fahrradwerke founded in 1907 in Sangerhausen. Incredulously Tim Moore rode one of these bikes for 9,000 kilometres (5,600 miles) across twenty European countries. In one example, he describes how he crossed from Romania to Serbia on the EV13 road across the spectacular Iron Gate dam; remember this was on a 20 inch wheeled, two geared folding shopping bike! His book reveals a cheeringly human story with, fortunately, a happy ending. Most escape bids from East Germany were breathless affairs involving barking German

Alsatian dogs and fatal bullets. However, the border-side village of Boseckendorf (in Germany) produced a more sedate drama: in 1961 and 1963 more than a quarter of its residents walked cheekily into the West completely undetected, when heavy snowfall buried the minefields and all but the top few feet of the fences. The residents simply walked over the fence - when opportunity knocks, take advantage! (Moore 2016)

In the continent of Africa, Cross is my favourite name for a river, conjuring up an image of angry white foam as it seeks to take its course to the coastline and its waters to the freedom of the sea. There is a bridge, barely seventy metres long, that separates Mfum in Nigeria on the west bank and Ekok on the Cameroon east bank. Alan Whelan in his book *African Brew Ha Ha* rode his motorbike across this rickety structure that was built by the British in 1946, thereby crossing the River Cross and reaching the custom officer post where he was invited inside. A secretary knocked and entered the room carrying a tiny teapot and two shot glasses in order to drink tea (not surprising by the book title, this is an ongoing theme in the book). The people in Mfum across the river are from the same tribe as the people in Ekok. To these tribespeople it is not a border, it is just a river that makes them really cross! On the Mali-Nigeria border, Alan Whelan answers the same questions that seem to occur on every other arduous border crossing, suggesting that one should print and laminate the answers to expedite the [border] crossings. In this case the border officials pointed him to the customs office where he could not believe his eyes: he thought he was delirious from the heat because in front of him was a car with a cow in the boot. The vehicle was not an estate or hatchback and the animal wasn't a calf but a fully grown cow. "It was in an ungainly position (which I suppose should go without saying), with its head and four hoofs hanging out the back like some ghastly pre-barbecue road show. How the hell did it get in there? Did they promise it a new life in Nigeria? Maybe the car is a shared taxi and the cow couldn't get a seat inside?" One thing was certain - the cow cleared customs much quicker than the author, Alan Whelan (Whelan 2010).

Tom Chesshyre tells the story of crossing the border between Tunisia and Libya (Chesshyre 2014), four months after the fall of Gaddafi. After handing over his passport and a letter of invitation from an oil company at the Tunisian border, not a lot happened for several hours apart from waiting in the open and getting covered in sand. When the penny dropped that money needed to be exchanged (basically, a bribe to a corrupt official), he walked through the whistling wind and passed a sign that said "La Tunisie vous souhaite bon voyage" (Tunisia wishes you a good journey). He travelled across no man's land to another sign that needed no translation: "Libya Free". Money helped again because the extra "passport fee" that he had previously paid in London meant that he bypassed the regular border kiosks. "Through a hole in a fence via a fistful of dinars" he had made it into the post-revolutionary country of Libya. Now he was a tourist in a land run by rebels with guns, entering the capital Tripoli where the guns were fired every night: "The hollow tap, tap, tap of bullets in the evening air" (Chesshyre 2014). Perhaps, this story makes you think that you do not want to cross borders, or possibly the opposite, drawing you into the excitement of a border crossing. If you want an exhilarating way to cross a border, why not try running across?

RUNNING ACROSS BORDERS

The courier Pheidippides (born 530BC – died 490 BC) did not realise that he would start a mass running trend when he was sent to Sparta to request help when the Persians landed at Marathon in Greece (from over the border in the area around Iran today). He ran about 240 kilometres (150 miles) in two days, and then ran back. After the battle he ran approximately 40 kilometres (26 miles) from the battlefield near Marathon to Athens to announce the Greek victory over Persia in the Battle of Marathon. With no great surprise to anyone who has ever attempted to run a marathon, sadly he collapsed and died. One of my favourite pastimes is jogging, somehow managing to run the London marathon five times for charitable causes. Fortunately, I did not suffer the same fate as Pheidippides, although in my last marathon when I was running uphill along Bird Cage Walk and passed Buckingham Palace approaching the finish line, I was beginning to wonder. With the memory of the pain of running fading fast, I considered the possibilities of running across different borders. The Istanbul Eurasian marathon is the only marathon in the world that crosses from one continent to another. The Istanbul Marathon starts on the Asian side of Istanbul and after 300 metres you run across the Bosporus Bridge to the continent of Europe but also in Istanbul. An interesting suggestion for a post run recovery would be an authentic Turkish hammam. So, if you like lots (and I mean lots) of soap suds to scrub your skin clean, it could complete a trip to the wonderful and cultural city of Istanbul. The bridge run is not the only inter-continental sporting first that has been held here. Venus Williams played a tennis game on the bridge in 2005 becoming the first tennis match to be played on two continents at the same time.

The relationship between Turkey and Greece has long been marked with hostilities (see chapter one), especially since the Cyprus invasion in 1974, but there is an encouraging run that signifies improved relations. There is a half marathon that started in Turkey's Edirne and ended in Greece's Kastanies, which demonstrates a positive step to more harmony between the two countries. In a rare gesture, Greece border guards do not ask the athletes for Schengen visas, normally required for any traveller entering the country from Turkey. Competitors jog a symbolic one kilometre-part of the half marathon inside Greek territory up to the town of Kastanies and return to the starting point in the border town of Edirne.

The last thing you need when you run a marathon is to stop, either for drinks or a toilet break, and certainly not to show travel documents. Fortunately, in the Bay of Fundy international marathon (Campobello Island, New Brunswick, Canada and Lubec, Maine, USA) you can run across the border because travel documents such as passports, visas are pre-cleared during the registration process. With a bib incorporating a timing chip, you can run across the border without stopping and as their marathon advertisement reviewed "even the border guards were cheering us on" - surely a rare occurrence! A run across the Widnes-Runcorn bridge (see Introduction) may be picturesque to a few die-hard UK northerners, but the Niagara Falls international marathon must be the most spectacular in the world. Runners cross into Canada from Buffalo, New York over the International Peace Bridge and then run along the scenic Niagara Parkway, ending at one of the world's most famous natural wonders, Niagara Falls. Spray jackets would probably be useful at the finish line. The Detroit International Marathon promotes the fact that their marathon course runs "through" water twice, first going over the Detroit River on the Ambassador Bridge from Detroit in Michigan to Windsor in Ontario. Then the race goes back under the river by running through the Detroit to Windsor Tunnel. Interestingly, the event organisers offer both an International half marathon and a USA only half marathon. Perhaps the latter is for runners who will not be allowed into Canada (see chapter six)!

There aren't many cross-border races in the world so you would not imagine one that crosses the contentious border between USA and Mexico (see chapter one). In spite of the political rhetoric of building a wall, there is a race that takes place between the border cities of El Paso in Texas and Juárez in Mexico. This race is a positive example of how the community around the longest border in the world can unite across an international boundary line. An extract from the organiser's website:

> "The Run International - The USA to Mexico 10K is more than a race. It's about the unique greatness of the largest borderland in the world. It illustrates how one community, united by an international boundary line, blends itself into one region."

It has a positive message illustrating how running and organising an international race can transcend boundaries and border issues. There is a different type of race that takes place near the USA to Mexico border. On the 5th of May 2001, two miles of barbed wire that divided the USA from Mexico were removed and replaced with white plastic fencing, remarkably the same type that you see on a horse racecourse. This fencing was to provide the centre line, not for the border between the countries, but for the Cinco de Mayo International Border Horse Race. It is extraordinary that this created the only horse race in the world that takes place simultaneously in two countries (Agua Prieta, Mexico and Douglas, Arizona, USA). Grandstands were set up on both sides of the border for spectators and approximately 20,000 people lined the track shouting to the spectators across the border. The Cinco de Mayo border races have continued to take place despite the increased security along the border, although with a different format. Because the border fence cannot be removed anymore, the horses run beside a three-metre barbed wire topped border wall. The Mexican horse runs on the Mexican side of the border and the USA horse runs on the USA side. Another optimistic example of how sport can transcend international boundaries (Shapiro 2004).

Horse racing and running are not the only sports to utilise the border between the USA and Mexico because in this location there is the most subversive game of volleyball in the world.

Affectionately known as "wallyball", this border sport is thought to have been first played as part of a Mexican fiesta in 1979, before being re-staged by a magazine editor in 2006. As the beach crowds cheer the ball crossing the border-wall they are promoting a political message, reducing the 2,000-mile border with the highest number of legal and illegal crossings in the world to just a sports net. This is a unique sporting match as both the Mexican and US teams are playing at home, with the fence as the neutral net. Of course, it is not perfect, as the spikes can be dangerous on the solid wall and lobs have to be much higher than a normal game of volleyball. Wallyball has gained fame and is now an annual April tradition in Naco, Arizona in USA and Naco, Sonora in Mexico. Other games of wallyball take place between Tijuana in Mexico and San Diego in California demonstrating how sport, again, can cut across political boundaries (Staufenberg 2015).

When you close your eyes and think of Monaco you might imagine many features such as sun, casinos, Princess Grace and motor racing. However, the Monaco Run must be one of the most beautiful and scenic marathon routes in the world. It runs through the impressive Principality of Monaco crossing two international borders, heading briefly into both France and Italy. So not only is this a stunning run but it also gives you the opportunity to see three countries in one running day.

Park runs have become phenomenally successful throughout the world for crowds of runners on a Saturday morning covering a distance of five kilometres (3.1 miles). Quirkily, some want to do two park runs in one day so some cities, like Sheffield, have a park run at 9am on New Year's Day and then the opportunity to do another run at 10 am at a nearby location. "Time Traveller park runners" is a nickname that enthusiasts have come up with for people who cross the International Date Line to complete two park runs in one day. If you are lucky enough to catch an aeroplane flight from Brisbane to Vancouver, for example, and cross the international dateline it can be completed in two different countries (Australia and Canada in this case). However, it would appear to be much easier and certainly less expensive to complete the two 5 kilometre runs in Sheffield!

When watching the London marathon runners in April, on the television, many viewers forget that most of the hard training mileage will have taken place in the depths of the British winter around December, January and February. However, the Cross-Border Challenge from England to Scotland is a local event that must be for very hardy runners only. Although it is merely a ten-kilometre route, it takes the runners from Carlisle in England to Gretna Green in Scotland…in the middle of January. This part of Britain is beautiful but not necessarily at its best at that time of the year. The advice, perhaps, is to combine it with a wedding in Gretna Green - now that would be an original and heart-warming idea (see chapter one for border crossings to Gretna Green). There is another cross-border race in the United Kingdom running from England to Wales. The Severn Bridge is also closed to traffic once a year to allow 2,500 people to take part in the Severn Bridge Half Marathon. It is a remarkable race as not only is the M48 motorway closed during the race, but the route also crosses from one country to another and back again. The 'old' bridge is an iconic landmark because it is open to the elements on all sides and with fantastic views, running between sea and sky! The bridge is also home to the Severn Bridge parkrun (as mentioned above), which is a free five kilometre run on every Saturday at 9.00am (see chapter one for Severn Bridge).

One of my other sporting interests is cricket and who else to write a border crossing story than Henry Blofeld, the former BBC radio commentator affectionately known as "Blowers" from the programme Test Match Special (Blofeld 2013). Blofeld's favourite border adventure happened in 1976. When he was scheduled to go to India to commentate on the cricket Test series, he decided to drive overland from London to Bombay (now Mumbai). He had four travellers with him, one of whom owned a 1921 Silver Ghost Rolls Royce, a most perfect claret-coloured motor car. They travelled in the Rolls Royce, through Europe and beyond to

Afghanistan, Iran and then Pakistan. They even had six tyres ordered for the car to be delivered to Tehran! They strapped the essential supplies to the outside of the car: cans of petrol and cases of Scotch whisky. After they got through the Khyber Pass (perhaps not to be advised today) they arrived at Peshawar and stayed at the Dean's Hotel, which is one of those famous old hotels that the English had a habit of leaving behind them. Rudyard Kipling and a young Winston Churchill were former guests. Unfortunately, the hotel has now been demolished and replaced with a concrete shopping plaza. They had stayed a short distance from the Indian border. It had taken them forty-six days and nights to reach Bombay. They always said that they would get there on the 22nd November in time for lunch, and, sure enough they sat down to lunch at a quarter to two, illustrating a remarkable piece of English punctuality! An outstanding travelling effort was demonstrated which characterised the appeal of the unique broadcaster Henry Blofeld.

CHAPTER 4
BORDER ERRORS / MAP WARS / MYSTERIES

The cool thing about being famous is travelling. I have always wanted to travel across seas, like to Canada and stuff.

BRITNEY SPEARS (BLENDER MAGAZINE 2004)

Maps became political weapons in the 17th and 18th centuries in a series of map wars between England and France. Guillaume Delisle, the son of a French map maker, produced over a hundred maps. He mapped the North American lands with the help of priests, fur traders and explorers and he was the first to focus on its interior. In 1718 Delisle produced a map which was controversial as it failed to acknowledge England's eastern colonies or Spanish claims north of the Rio Grande. In 1733, Henry Popple, an English cartographer produced the first large-scale map of North America; he was one map maker who realised the importance of accurate, or even strategically inaccurate, mapping. Rather than using violence, politicians were starting to use cartographers and their maps to push for expansion of their own borders and to reduce their enemy's territory.

The sun never sets on the British Empire was a boast which suggested that if you kept moving you could be in sunshine and still be in parts of the atlas that were coloured pink: in other words territories ruled or administered by the United Kingdom. In theory at the start of the 20th century, you could travel the Empire from Australia to Canada to large parts of Africa, through to India, Ceylon (Sri Lanka) and to Malaya, although the quickest way to visit all these at the time would have been by sailing ship. At its zenith the British Empire covered over 35 million square kilometres (13 million square miles and 25% of the world's land surface) and 26% of the world's population. To put it into context, the Roman and Ottoman empires were only about 5 million square kilometres (1.9 million square miles) put together. To govern such a vast area of the globe, Britain set up separate colonies (later dominions) with an army and a governor who was a representative of the king or queen or empress. In order to maintain law and order within its borders and build roads and railways, accurate maps were needed. An example of the need for accurate maps comes from the East India Company who commissioned map makers such as Rennell and Lambton to carry out a trigonometrical survey. The principle was to mark out a line between two fixed points to achieve an accurate baseline. The surveyor uses a theodolite (a low power telescope mounted on a tripod) to measure the angle between one end of the baseline pole and the other. The mapmaker is trying to ascertain the length of one side of a triangle and two angles. Using basic trigonometry, he or she could calculate the length of the other two sides. By repeating this process, the surveyor measures the ground in a series of zig-zagging triangles. The larger the triangles the faster the mapping, although there are likely to be more errors. It would be more accurate if there were smaller triangles. In fact, the ground is seldom flat so only small triangles may be possible in mountainous areas. A very large theodolite would be needed to complete the mapping, for example Lambton's was the size of a small tractor and weighed over half a ton.

In 1830 there was a surveyor-general who acquired the most

accurate surveying instruments and completed a massive survey from the Himalayas to the most southern part of India (Cape Comorin). Whilst surveying, he suffered malaria, dysentery, bouts of paralysis and even spells of madness. Everyone now knows his name, though perhaps not that he was a surveyor. His successor Andrew Waugh announced that, through triangulation, he had discovered the highest mountain in the world and called it Peak XV. He later re-named the peak in honour of his predecessor: George Everest. Everest objected to the honour as he had nothing to do with its discovery and it was a name difficult to pronounce in Hindi. In fact, his name was pronounced "EEV-rest" little did I know that geography teachers throughout the world were pronouncing the highest mountain in the world incorrectly!

Cyril John Radcliffe dragged his pen across a map of India, a place he had never seen, in fact he had never been east of Paris, and cleaved two countries from one. This was suggested in W.H. Auden's poem *Partition* "Having never set eyes on the land he was called to partition". Radcliffe was given the chairmanship of the two boundary committees set up with the passing of the Indian Independence Act. To be fair to him, Radcliffe did not want the job and other officials were probably not queuing up for it either. He was faced with the daunting task of drawing the borders for the new nations of Pakistan and India in a way that would leave as many Hindus and Sikhs in India as possible and leave the majority of Muslims in Pakistan. Radcliffe submitted his partition map on 9 August 1947, which split Punjab and Bengal almost in half. The new boundaries involved separating 80 million people and dividing up more than 450,000 square kilometres (174,000 square miles) of land to carve a bisected Pakistan – a West Pakistan and an East Pakistan (which from 1971 was known as Bangladesh). So, Pakistan became two non-contiguous enclaves separated geographically by India. Radcliffe's efforts culminated in over fourteen million people, approximately seven million from each side, fleeing across the border when they discovered that the new boundaries left them in the "wrong" country. The first-hand experience of Bapsi Sidhwa in *Cracking India* (Sidhwa 1988) illustrates the chaos caused by the largest and most terrible exchange of population known to history. She discusses how sectarian violence soon escalated and riots broke out amongst the city of Lahore's once harmonious people. The novel is generally referred to as a story about the Partition of India, but its original title was *Ice Candy Man* which allows for broader interpretation of the story. There was very little sweetness between the Muslim, Hindu, Sikh, Parsee and Christian groups. After seeing the mayhem occurring on both sides of the boundary with the largest mass migration of people in human history, over fourteen million people displaced, a refugee crisis and violence, it was no surprise that Radcliffe decided to reject his salary of 40,000 rupees (then 3,000 pounds).

India's far north-east region is divided from the rest of India, not by a wall or a fence but by Radcliffe's clumsy pen, which nearly severed the north-east from "mainland" India. Only a tiny strip of territory, twenty-one kilometres (thirteen miles) across at its narrowest point, keeps the north-east from being pinched off altogether. Indians call the corridor the "Chicken's Neck". The Indo-Bangladesh border is a famous fence consisting of three layers of barbed wire, concrete pillars and rolls of concertina or razor wire. Bangladesh and India share a 4,156 kilometre long (2,582 miles) international border, the fifth-longest land border in the world. India signed an agreement with Bangladesh after 1971 forbidding either nation from building a "defensive structure" within 150 metres of the actual border or "zero line". This is the case for most of its route. However, in some areas the natural landforms such as cliffs and rivers make this buffer zone so difficult to stick to that the barrier runs inside the 150 metres zone. This barrier runs close to a most memorable place for geography students – Cherrapunji – which, for some reason everyone seems to know, has the world's highest rainfall. Except it does not; apparently a nearby village called Mawsynram has the official highest rainfall title according to the *Guinness Book of World Records.* North-east India also boasts other world records such as the world's hottest chilli pepper, the Bhut Jolokia or "Ghost Chilli" and in 2009 a woman from Gauhati ate a record 51 of them in two minutes. Hot stuff and afterwards I bet she felt like drinking the 12 metres of rainfall falling in Cherrapunji that day! Perhaps it is something about the border barrier in this area which makes people do odd things, because there is a man in Assam who collects poisonous spiders so he can eat a thousand of them in one day! Radcliffe had a lot to answer for, although it was not all his fault. With reason, Indians are still fuming about the nature of the slapdash line, the British government's arrogance, sloppiness of the boundary and lack of concern for people along the line.

The disputed state of Jammu and Kashmir, once a separate monarchy, lies between India, Pakistan and China. Both Pakistan and India claimed Kashmir and they were at war over its sovereignty in 1965 until there was a ceasefire which placed India in control of southern Kashmir, and Pakistan in control of north-western Kashmir. The respective claimants issued maps denying the other's territory claim, for example in 1984 a Pakistani government tourist map included Kashmir in Pakistan. In response, the Indian government did the same by including part of Kashmir in India (Monmonier 1996). British and American atlases have consistently issued notes stating, for instance, that an area occupied by India is claimed by Pakistan and vice versa. Publishers have found it difficult to export the same atlases to each of the countries concerned. The issue is not just with published books because online mapmakers can simply change the world's borders according to where they are being viewed. In Pakistan, Kashmir appears disputed while in India, it shows as a part of India. Amazingly, Google Maps changes disputed borders based on what country you search from!

There are many mysteries relating to maps and their errors, some highlighted today with the use of increasing technology. With over eighty percent market share in mobile maps and over a billion users, Google Maps has a disproportionate impact on people's perception of the world such as driving directions, restaurant reviews and, more importantly, adjudicating historical border wars. As with Kashmir (above), when it comes to contested borders, people in different countries often see different things. The body of water between Japan and the Korean Peninsula is known as, to almost all, the Sea of Japan but for Google apps users in South Korea, it is listed as the East Sea. More than 4,000 miles away, the waterway separating Iran from Saudi Arabia may be either the Persian Gulf or the Arabian Gulf, depending on who is looking online. And the line in Western Sahara marking the northern border with Morocco disappears for Moroccans seeking it out on the world wide web — along with the region's name altogether! The sparsely populated north-west Africa region is disputed between Morocco, which seized it in 1975, and the indigenous Sahrawi (see chapter seven).

The origins of an international dispute between Nicaragua and Costa Rica can be traced back to a Google Maps error. On the online website, the territory was shown as belonging to Costa Rica although it was really Nicaragua's land. As a result, Nicaraguan troops crossed the border into Costa Rica, removed that country's flag, and replaced it with one of their own flags. Nicaragua asked Google to keep the border line as it is, while Costa Rica asked for the border to be changed back to the way it was. The situation was tense, to say the least, until the U.N. Security Council intervened to mediate and solve this border dispute.

When territory disappears, it can be stressful for people and communities alike. With global warming, many low-lying islands could tragically disappear as sea levels rise. Google Maps seems to have predicted this scenario by causing two French islands off the coast of Newfoundland, Saint-Pierre and Miquelon, to be submerged. Fortunately, they reappeared on Google Maps when the error was publicised. According to the internet, for about a month in the summer of 2010 the settlement called Sunrise, Florida, no longer existed. All its public buildings, addresses, phone numbers and public spaces were missing from World Wide Web searches. The reason was that when the search-engine was used for Sunrise in Florida, Google Maps redirected users two hundred miles away to Sarasota, Florida instead (Garfield 2012).

In 1909 the *General Map of Africa* mapped by Edward Hertslet was published, seven years after he died, using border colours to distinguish British possessions and protectorates from those of France, Italy, Germany and Portugal, Belgium and the Independent States. It represented the result of the "Scramble for Africa" (Pakenham 1990) which brought virtually all of the continent under foreign domination by the end of the nineteenth century. The supposed aim of the West Africa Conference held in Berlin (1884-1885) was to uphold David Livingstone's mission to bring commerce, Christianity and civilisation to the peoples of Africa. It was convened by the German Chancellor Otto von Bismarck in order to resolve border disputes between European powers. After the Congress, he spoke of the "careful solicitude" that the signatories had shown for the welfare of the indigenous people in drafting this resultant General Act. With respect, if solicitude means care and concern, then the opposite took place. The principle established at the Berlin Conference was that the hinterland of the stretch of coast occupied by the European powers could be included under their sphere of influence. Basically, it meant that land could be taken and claimed according to how far explorers and military forces had advanced on the ground. The diplomats must have been in a large room because they studied a five-metre high wall map of Africa when they were dividing up the territories. Many Africans are now prisoners of the political geography set up by the European powers (at the Berlin Conference) and the natural barriers of the African continent. So tribal areas that were bound together by common culture and language were broken up. Cecil Rhodes dreamt of British colonies running from Cairo in Egypt through British East Africa (Kenya), Northern Rhodesia (Zambia), Southern Rhodesia (Zimbabwe), Bechuanaland (Botswana) to the

Cape of Good Hope in South Africa. His dream of a north to south linkage railway was thwarted by Germany's colonisation of Tanzania. Some examples from the Berlin Conference are: France annexed Chad (French West Africa); Italy took Somalia; Portugal dominated Angola. Where anomalies appeared on the map, they served the needs of the colonial powers rather than the native population. Many of the ethnic conflicts that are evident in Africa today can be traced back to the colonial legacy and that Conference in Berlin.

Leopold II, King of the Belgians was known for his prodigious appetite - for example, eating two entire roast pheasants in a Paris restaurant. It is no surprise to hear that he used a culinary metaphor when declaring his determination to obtain the largest possible slice of what he called "the magnificent African cake". At the Berlin Conference in 1885 he secured his own private colony which was seventy-five times larger than Belgium! Leopold was the founder and sole owner of the Congo Free State, a private project undertaken on his own behalf (the present-day Democratic Republic of the Congo). In Berlin 1885, the colonial nations of Europe authorised his claim by committing the Congo Free State to improving the lives of the native inhabitants. Leopold ignored these conditions and ran the Congo using the mercenary Force Publique for his personal gain. He extracted a fortune from the territory, initially by the collection of ivory, and after a rise in the price of rubber in the 1890s, by forced labour from the native population to harvest and process rubber. When he was sixty-five, Leopold took as a mistress Caroline Lacroix, a sixteen-year-old French prostitute! She was deeply unpopular in Belgium to say the least, bragging that she spent three million francs on dresses at a single store in Paris in one visit. Caroline once complained to Leopold that the evening express train back to Brussels gave her little time to shop, causing Leopold to arrange it so that the train would leave an hour later. Leopold lavished upon her large sums of money, estates, gifts from the Congo and a noble title, Baroness Vaughan. It is no wonder that later she became known as Queen of the Congo.

Leopold's riches from the Congo were not benefiting his country, but rather himself and his young mistress. I know it is a well-worn phrase, but Leopold certainly wanted his cake as well as wanting to eat it; apparently, he was related to Marie-Antoinette after all (see the pedicle of DR Congo in chapter five).

With respect to the problem area of Darfur, Jason McCue a human rights lawyer visited the area. He was asked to explain the region spiralling out of control and the genocide happening in Darfur. He explained the slow progress that has been made in Sudan's Comprehensive Peace Agreement (CPA) which ended Africa's longest-running civil war in 2005. He explained ethnic issues between Muslim Africans and Muslim Arabs, tribal feuds and conflict between nomadic and farmstead farmers. It was all too confusing. McCue then recalled something an old Turkish farmer said to him when he (McCue) was lost, trying to find a small road crossing somewhere on a Turkish mountain. The farmer laughed at him when he was shown the road detailed on the map and retorted: "It doesn't exist, it's just government ink." That is the heart of the problem. The borders between Sudan, Chad, Central African Republic (CAR) and Democratic Republic of the Congo (DRC) are just that: "Government ink" (Hutton 2018).

I taught my final geography lesson after almost twenty-five years of teaching, fourteen of those in a school in Derbyshire, but it wasn't my last educational duty. We had been raising money to fund a school trip for two years with a series of cake stalls, tombolas and supermarket packing. The trip was organised by the local council and the British Exploring Society, but it was not to study the likes of coastal erosion at Lulworth Cove or tourism in the Lake District National Park. This was no ordinary school trip, we were going to help and teach in an African school, as well as camping and trekking in the Namibian desert. The trip would also give me the chance to study the former German South West Africa's (now Namibia) borders. Some of these boundary lines were classic examples of where anomalies appear on a map of Africa. The narrow Caprivi Strip in the north-eastern corner of Namibia looks like a map error until you realise that it was created to give the ex-German colony access to the Zambezi river. You might have noticed the Caprivi Strip on a globe or atlas because it is that 450 kilometres (280 miles) panhandle of Namibia stretching improbably eastward towards Zimbabwe. Of all the weird African borders caused by the colonial carve-up of the 19th century, Caprivi is one of the quirkiest. It is one of the most glamorously named, since it has also been called "Itenge" or "the Okavango Panhandle," adventurous-sounding names straight from a Michael Crichton novel or James Bond film. You can argue that the Caprivi Strip was an accident because it only exists because someone forgot about the largest waterfall in the world. Leo von Caprivi was the German politician who succeeded Otto von Bismarck (chair of the Berlin Conference on Africa) as chancellor in 1890. His administration signed an agreement trading the islands of Zanzibar to the British in exchange for Heligoland, an archipelago just north-west of Hamburg. Germany also negotiated what they thought was a bonus, this little strip of Bechuanaland, no wider than 30 kilometres across in some places. The Germans wanted the strip because it ended at the Zambezi River which would provide a route to the Indian Ocean and Germany's East African territories (modern-day Tanzania, Rwanda, and Burundi). However, the German negotiators should firstly have checked a map. In fact, the Zambezi River is difficult to navigate along the Caprivi Strip due to rapids. Then, 60 kilometres (37 miles) east of Caprivi, it becomes extremely non-navigable due to a 110-metre drop called the Victoria Falls. Not only was one of the world's largest waterfalls in the way but it was named after their rival's (Britain's) empress! The Caprivi Strip turned out to be useless for minerals and trade and Bismarck was more than dismayed that Germany had traded away its entire "trousers for a button" (Jennings 2013). So why not change the African borders drawn with a pen and ruler and such little sympathy for local people? The Organisation of African Unity met in 1963 to discuss border changes on the continent. The Organisation recognised the de facto state borders acknowledging that any attempt to redraw the boundaries would once again lead to bloodshed. Much of Africa's history of political instability, debt and famine can be traced back to the decisions made around a table in Berlin in 1885 (Clark 2016).

President John F Kennedy addressed residents of the USA with a serious foreign policy issue - not Vietnam or Cuba as one might expect, but Laos. Rather like a sad geography teacher using a Powerpoint presentation for the very first time, JFK showed a series of three maps. You could see how the red tide of the communists from North Vietnam (backed by the Soviet Union) would swamp the country of Laos and create a "domino effect" across the whole of Asia. The mapping technique demonstrated power and understanding of the issue and the implication is one of control. To illustrate the effectiveness of JFK's address, troops were deployed to the area, and Khrushchev of the Soviet Union backed down. His successor, Lyndon B Johnson, had many more maps to show to the American people demonstrating how badly the Vietnam war was going. Of course, these maps were never shown!

Plato's conundrum, Captain Nemo's quandary, and the riddle of the journey to the "centre" of the earth are so easily "solved". Apparently, the co-ordinates to find Atlantis are well known: 31 15'15.53N, 24 15'30.53W (600 miles west of Morocco, deep in the Atlantic Ocean near the Canary Islands). Users often believe that Google Earth is definitive but in terms of Atlantis no one knows the correct answer. Most accounts tend to place Atlantis somewhere in or near the Atlantic Ocean, with placement ranging from near the Bermuda Triangle all the way to islands in the Mediterranean Sea near Greece and Italy. Many believe Dr Erlinsson's idea that the country of Ireland is Atlantis, although his book's sub-title does not inspire confidence: *Mapping the Faery Land*. Kircher's map from 1665 shows Atlantis almost filling the North Atlantic, basing his map on the Greek philosopher Plato's description. A map of the Aegean Sea shows Thera (now Santorini) in the Cyclades group of Mediterranean islands which was the site of one of the largest volcanic eruptions ever, about 3,600 years ago, with the power equivalent to 6,000 hydrogen bombs. The tsunami that followed led to the destruction of the island's Minoan civilisation and allegedly inspired Plato's story and possible location of Atlantis.

I flew into Perth, Australia in order to watch the last ever Ashes cricket test match to be played at the WACA ground. Sightseeing time involved searching for Margaret River on a map which I realised was a town rather than just a river or a label shown on a bottle of wine. There was also a place that I was interested in called Wittenoom which I struggled to find on any map even with, as an ex-geography teacher, hopefully above average map-reading skills. Wittenoom is located 1425 kilometres (885 miles) north of Perth in the state of Western Australia. The reason I couldn't find this place was because Wittenoom had been wiped from the map in 2007 by the state government, or one could call it degazetted (meaning to remove its official status). Whatever name the process is given, the town's name was removed from official maps and road signs. During the 1950s and early 1960s Wittenoom was Australia's only supplier of blue asbestos (Fletcher 2018). The mine was shut down in 1966 due to unprofitability and growing health concerns from asbestos mining and inhalation of asbestos fibres in the area. Of the 20,000 people that lived and worked in the region, it is believed that 2,000 have died from mesothelioma from blue asbestos dust. Some people believe that the area can never be made entirely safe for human habitation. The reason it was taken off the map, is that Wittenoom is perhaps the most contaminated site in whole of the Southern Hemisphere and has previously been labelled "Australia's Chernobyl" (Foster 2019).

Maps can often be mysterious and betray your plans. In 1981, the police in Arizona were hunting a man who had committed a series of crimes associated with fraud and bigamy. The accused man had married a series of unsuspecting women but then stole large sums of jewellery and cash from his newly married brides. The charming and good-looking (well, he must have been) Giovanni Vigliotto claimed to have married over 105 women over several years, without ever divorcing most of them. In court, he said that the figure was a joke that he had made, but authorities then confirmed at least 82 marriages in nine states in such countries as Canada, United Kingdom, Italy and Hong Kong. He was certainly a border-hopping gigolo especially as he proposed to most of his future wives on the first date! The only reason he was convicted, and therefore sentenced to 34 years in prison, was because he left an annotated map (with all his wives on it) at the house of one of his abandoned wives (Monmonier 1996).

Map blunders make amusing anecdotes especially when the media reports on the most outrageous mistakes. An example comes from the 1960s when the press reported that the American Automobile Association had accidentally omitted the country's twenty-third largest city in the USA from its road map. Headlines such as "Lost Seattle" did not help the map editors who perhaps were sleepless after the very expensive recall and reprinting of the maps (Monmonier 1996). The Canadian government tourist office printed an airline map in a brochure to attract British tourists to the Great White North as they called it; unfortunately, they missed off an important city – their capital called Ottawa. Not surprisingly, the residents of Ottawa were very annoyed especially with the explanation that the map was printed before the New York to Ottawa point of entry air service had started. This clarification still doesn't make a lot of sense to many of the population. Calgary, Regina and even Winnipeg were included on their map but not the capital. As the manager of Ottawa's Capital Visitors and Convention Bureau exclaimed, "Ottawa should be shown in any case, even if the only point of entry was by a two-person kayak."

The Turtle Islands lying in the Sulu Sea can be distinguished between the Philippine islands (Tawi-Tawi) and the Malaysian counterpart (Taganak). Access is difficult which is no bad thing as it keeps the egg poachers away because, not surprisingly, the island is famous for excellent turtle breeding grounds. At one point, these islands were affected by someone's poor map reading skills, leading to an international incident. In 1988 the press in Manila, the capital of the Philippines, reported the Malaysian annexation of the

Turtle Islands. This promoted three days of media hysteria as news maps showed the Malaysian encroachment onto the islands. However, these maps were traced back to the erroneous reading of an American navigation chart by a Philippine naval officer. He mistook a line representing the recommended deep-water route for ships passing the Turtle Islands for the boundary of Malaysia's newly declared exclusive economic zone (Monmonier 1996). "What a mistake-a to make-a!" as Alberto Bertorelli would say in the television programme 'Allo 'Allo.

The invasion of Grenada by USA soldiers highlighted how modern warfare was equally susceptible to cartographic errors and mistakes. In 1983, after the government was overthrown in a coup, there were approximately six hundred American medical students who needed rescuing from Grenada and an air attack took place. However, the only map intelligence the troops had were a few out of date British maps and a tourist map (with hastily drawn military grids). Air attack commenced, destroying a mental health hospital that was not shown on these maps. Another air strike, ordered by a commander on the ground using a different set of coordinates to the grid coordinates of the strike planes, unfortunately killed one soldier and wounded eighteen more. The use of accurate maps was shown to be so important, especially if you have military aircraft involved!

Schools have various and often ingenious methods of obtaining resources for teaching. Geography teachers, for example, always follow the restrictive-copyright rules when photocopying (honestly)! Of course, copyright infringement may arise if maps, for instance, are copied from a single original work. Suing by publishers can be a lucrative source of money if it can be proved. What can map publishers do? They have been known to deliberately falsify their maps by adding "trap streets". These deliberate errors are usually placed subtly in remote locations which are less likely to confuse the map user. One example is from the 1970s when Mount Richard appeared on a county map in Boulder, Colorado. This falsity was not discovered for two years and only then traced back to be the work of Richard Ciacci, a draughtsman in the local public works department (Monmonier 1996). It may be worth looking closely at maps in order find out if there are any more cartographers who have placed mischievous features on published maps!

CHAPTER 5
TO BE AN ENCLAVE OR AN EXCLAVE

Some definitions are clear and simple: exclave and enclave meanings are not straightforward. An exclave is a slice of one country's territory not attached to the rest of it: it is surrounded entirely by another country. A "pene-exclave", such as Gibraltar, Alaska or Northern Ireland, is partially surrounded by water (the word *pene* means almost). An enclave is territory that is surrounded totally by a foreign territory. An enclave in one nation may also be an exclave of another. Thus Lesotho, which is surrounded entirely by South Africa, is an enclave, but not an exclave as there is no Lesothoan motherland. Whereas Kaliningrad on the shores of the Baltic is an exclave of Russia but, since it borders two countries (and the sea), it is not, technically, an enclave. I hope this explanation is understandable; I am sure it is as clear as mud!

Enclaves and exclaves play a very important role in world affairs often providing an immovable historical dispute or the blue touch paper for a new argument. Some of their world locations are so famous that they provide bywords for wars, stand-offs and misery: Berlin, Ceuta, Melilla, Dubrovnik, Gaza Strip, Gibraltar, Kaliningrad and Transnistria. You would imagine that globalisation would reduce the number of these irregularities on the map, but there seems to be an opposite trend. Many more enclaves and exclaves were created in the late twentieth century than were removed from maps. The dismantling of Yugoslavia and the Soviet Union in the early 1990s introduced over twenty new ones in Europe and west Asia (Parker 2010).

Gambia is an enclave which is inside Senegal. The enclave is described variously, and usually unflatteringly, as having the shape of a worm or tongue. The British clung to this piece of land in French West Africa in the hope of exploiting the Gambia River, considered to be one of the most easily navigable rivers in Africa. However, the hope of using the river to its full potential was never realised. The five London charity marathons have taken their toll on my knees, but I still aspire to cross the borders of countries when jogging. The Gambia could offer the potential to run from its northern border to its southern border because it is only fifteen miles wide. Nevertheless, the lack of bridges on the river Gambia, which flows east to west, may not help this border to border country run. Remarkably, the country's present boundaries were defined in 1889 after an agreement between the United Kingdom and France. It is often claimed by Gambians that the distance between its north and south borders corresponds to the area that a British naval cannon at the time could reach from the river Gambia's channel. A fantastical story, and there is no historical evidence to support it. The border was delineated using careful surveying methods by the Franco-British boundary commission. Apart from its coastline, where the Gambia borders the Atlantic Ocean, it is an enclave of Senegal and is by far the smallest country (only 300 miles / 483 kilometres long) on mainland Africa.

A quadripoint is a point on the Earth that touches four distinct regions such as the meeting of four borders. Technically, there is no quadripoint involving international borders of four countries. While the joining of three nations is quite common, no four countries meet at a single point. However, nothing tends to be simple in geography. The closest example of a quadripoint is the border between Namibia, Zambia, Zimbabwe and Botswana near the confluence of the Zambezi river with the Chobe River near Kazungula (refer to the Caprivi Strip in chapter four). In reality, it is not a quadripoint but two tripoints which lie only 300 metres from each other. This may appear as a quadripoint on a map of a lower resolution, but a higher resolution map shows this not to be true. The existence or non-existence of this quadripoint may just be an interesting piece of geography trivia in a pub quiz, but it has been a matter of life and death in the region. In 1970, both Rhodesia (now Zimbabwe), and South Africa which then controlled modern-day Namibia, claimed that the quadripoint did exist, and that therefore the Kazungula ferry connecting Zambia and Botswana, an important passage for almost a century, was illegal. Shots were fired at the ferry, and one boat was even sunk by the Rhodesian army! The current legal consensus is that the two tripoints here might possibly meet at one single spot in the middle of the Zambezi river but a boundary survey is needed. I understand that this scenario is unlikely to be agreed by the four countries involved in the near future.

If the Namibia-Zambia-Zimbabwe-Botswana quadripoint is mistaken, it means that there was only ever one point that was truly shared by four nations. This point existed briefly in late 1960 and early 1961, in central Africa. For only eight months, Cameroon, Chad, Nigeria, and a little-known British territory called Northern Cameroon (also called, rather confusingly, Northern Cameroons) met in the middle of Lake Chad, near the floating island of Kaalom. Unfortunately for border spotters, Nigeria took over Northern Cameroon(s) in May 1961 becoming the Sardauna Province, and the elusive quadripoint was lost to the world forever (Jennings 2004).

So, although there are no primary (international) quadripoints, there are few examples of secondary quadripoints where there is the meeting of borders of four states or administrative regions of a country. The convergence of the US states of Utah, Colorado, New Mexico and Arizona is the most famous secondary quadripoint, better known as "The Four Corners". The monument that lies at this spot is not only the point in the USA where four states meet, but as their boundaries were designated along parallel lines, the states meet at right angles as well!

Another border-spotter's exciting event is where two nations form a rare four-sided border at the peak of a mountain. Technically not a quadripoint, the town of Jungholz is still a freakish geographical anomaly. It is located in Austria in the state of Tyrol and is only accessible via Germany. There are few places so geographically curious as a single point at the top of Mount Sorgschrofen. Here, the borders meet at a small point at the summit of the mountain, extending in four directions down its slopes, forming quadrants of Germany (to the East and West) and Austria (to the North and South). Strangely, when viewed from above, as on a political map, the borders look like crosses. So, while according to maps, Jungholz is not officially surrounded by Germany thanks to this lone mountaintop, her human inhabitants cannot physically travel from their homes to the rest of their country without leaving Austria (Parker 2010).

An interesting location in Germany and another good question for any geography teacher to set the students giggling is where is Wank Mountain? Nearby is the 'magical forest' of Zauberwald where local legend suggests that God bade the angels distribute all the things of beauty equally throughout the world. The angels gathered up in their gowns in the mountains and seas, the rivers, lakes, trees and flowers but two of them paused to admire the beautiful things that they had carried, and when the Lord saw this he let them enjoy their wonder for a while and then reminded them to be on their way. The two angels were so startled by the voice of God that they dropped the folds of their gowns and all the beautiful things fell out in a cascade and landed in one spot, which is known as Berchtesgadener Land. On a map, Berchtesgadener Land takes the shape of an arrowhead about one-quarter of the size of Andorra (470 square kilometres or 180 square miles) inserted into Austria. This enclave is crammed with mountains including Watzmann, the highest peak in Germany. It was a separate state ruled by its own provosts until it was annexed by Bavaria in 1803. Across the border in Austria, a boy called Schicklgruber grew up in a small place called Braunau eventually moving to Vienna and taking over a political party. To cut a very long story short, he moved the party's headquarters onto a mountain called Obersalzberg in Berchtesgadener Land, buying Haus Wachenfeld – the *Berghof* – with the royalties of his book, *Mein Kampf.* No other mountain border area has inspired such terrible deeds, such as the plans for the Third Reich in the 1930s. "It was there that all my great projects were conceived and ripened" wrote Adolph Hitler. He spent more time in this chalet than anywhere else during the Second World War, but there is no point try finding it today. On 25th April 1945, 318 Lancaster bombers dropped 1,243 tons of bombs onto the area around his chalet, the last refuge of the Third Reich (Crane 1996).

I offer an example of a simple GCSE geography question, when does a village become a town? Perhaps not such a simple answer if you live in Llivia, a place that has become a small Spanish town stuck in the middle of France. In 1659 when the Treaty of the Pyrenees was signed, Spain ceded thirty-three villages in the north of Cerdanya to France. The French claimed to have been cheated out of Llivia by a cunning and calculated Spanish manoeuvre. After signing the treaty, Madrid deemed Llivia to be a town, not a village. A 'cunning plan' by Spain, as Baldrick in *Blackadder* would say. So Llivia still retains Spanish legislation, economy and taxes. Dialling codes are Spanish as are the police and while it is part of Spain, its locals are still fiercely Catalan and primarily speak Catalan as well as Spanish. So do not expect to recognise the signage in this town as traditionally Spanish. Remarkably, access between Spain and Llivia is by a 'neutral road' administered in turn by both France and Spain on a six-monthly rota with Llivia jutting out like a Gibraltarian promontory over the valley.

A link to both Spain and the UK is the British Overseas Territory of Gibraltar. It is located at the entrance of the Mediterranean Sea, at the southern end of the Iberian Peninsula, sharing a land border with Spain. It also has a coastal border, so therefore it can be classed as a pene-exclave (almost). The territory was ceded to Britain in 1713 after it was captured in 1704. Today, the small airport is well known to have its landing strip pass through the main street of the city, so with every take-off or landing, cars must clear the road! A friend who was a Gibraltar resident working in the online betting industry (presumably like so many others for tax reasons), tells the story of approaching the border with Spain at the crossing point called La Linea. In the toilets were naked women strapping cigarettes to their bodies, in order to smuggle them across the border, presumably after getting dressed again.

In another location, a few of the women who are wearing djellabas of different colours, cross the borders of Melilla and Ceuta to Morocco, with smuggled goods. Each colour of their attire represents their marital status with, for example, dark brown representing being single. These two Spanish cities (Melilla and Ceuta), 250 miles (400 kilometres) apart, are located on the Mediterranean coast of Morocco. Ceuta was ceded to Spain as early as 1668, while the Spanish borders of Melilla were established in the 19th century. They are two small enclaves of Spain forming the European Union's only land borders with Africa. There is huge pressure by African refugees who want to enter the cities, so the Spanish government have built fences to a height of three metres with barbed wire, watchtowers, patrols as well as other more advanced technological means to stop immigration. The coast is also patrolled with guard ships to stop illegal migrants and drug runners. Morocco is renowned for growing marijuana reputedly producing up to half the world's supply in the Rif mountains to the north of the country. The demand for a blend of tobacco and marijuana (called kif) in this part of the world is high. So it is possible here, although illegal, to smoke kif from the Rif mountains!

The thorny issues of the exclaves and enclaves in Gibraltar, Ceuta and Melilla are ongoing (especially with the UK leaving the EU in 2020), but Great Britain has a series of outliers, necks and strange bedfellows within its own borders. The Maelor is an area of north-east Wales along the border with England. The name Maelor is an old Welsh word translated as "land of the prince" from *mael* "prince" and *llawr* "low ground". The area and television signal masts stick out into England, so that when a programme was made about this place, no one in Maelor could watch it. The Maelor has been an exclave of Flintshire ever since Edward I gave it as a gift to his wife Eleanor of Aquitaine. It is rather like an English island in Wales but far away from the sea. A friend has a farm on the Welsh border, and he has fields in England and two fields in Wales. He said, jokingly I hope, that he would have a place to go if war ever broke out between England and Wales (Parker 2010). In 1996 a local government reorganisation took place, and Maelor became part of the new unitary authority called the county borough of Wrexham, to many people's dismay (at least Wrexham can boast that it has the picturesque Bangor-on-Dee racecourse nearby).

The counties of England have many exclaves outside the main county borders such as Dudley in the Midlands. Dudley is a market town with an interesting zoo nearby. The town has much potential, although its commercial centre has suffered strong competition from the nearby Merry Hill shopping centre. The centre must have been incorrectly named because surely one can never be merry in a modern shopping-mall? For many years the town, but strangely not Dudley Castle, was outside the boundary of Staffordshire forming part of an exclave of the county of Worcestershire.

Scotland has some even more remarkable outliers in the county of Cromartyshire. It consisted of the area around the old county town of Cromarty and no less than twenty-two separate enclaves and exclaves, transferred from Ross-shire in the late 17th century. It is as though these parcels of land had been strewn across the whole of Scotland by a bearded giant. The largest part, six times the size of the old shire, is Coigach, north-west from Ullapool which covers 183 square miles. The other twenty-one exclaves varied in size from twenty-eight square miles to one that was only fifty-one acres at the tip of the uninhabited Gruinard Island. The island gained notoriety in the Second World War as the place where anthrax was tested on sheep (Parker 2010). Whilst a visit to Cromarty would be highly recommended, it is perhaps best to still avoid the island of Gruinard.

One of my cherished pastimes is to drink a pint of bitter called "Dizzy Blonde" (which probably reveals a lot about the man who drinks it) especially in my favourite national park called the Peak District. Near the charming village of Tideswell is a public house peculiarly called "The Ship". This pub, allegedly, is the furthest pub from the coast in England so the landlord must have had a sense of humour. Incidentally another amusingly titled pub is on the coast in Portsmouth, called the "Jolly Taxpayer". I have always been interested in where the centre of places are; the centre of Great Britain is Dunsop Bridge, Lancashire (historically the village was in the West Riding of Yorkshire but no need to go over again the changes to county boundaries in 1972 - see introduction). The town of Haltwhistle in Northumberland claims the same title by another calculation and has banners stating that it is the "Centre of Britain". Of course, the centre of the UK will be different because it includes Northern Ireland. However, my advice is not to go there because the centre of the UK is in the middle of the sand banks on Morecambe Bay, apparently!

Returning to the Derbyshire pub, there was a local quiz with the question "How many Stans are there in the world?" Assuming that the question refers to countries, not people called Stanley, the answer was seven, all in Asia, and it means "place of" or "country" in the Persian/Urdu/Farsi languages. The Ferghana Valley is in central Asia, nearly 1,250 miles (2,000 kilometres) from the nearest ocean at the crossroads of three former Soviet states Kyrgyzstan, Uzbekistan and Tajikistan. The valley contains no less than eight enclaves. It consists of two marooned outposts of Tajikistan and four bits of Uzbekistan in that part of the valley that is in Kyrgyzstan, as well as one Tajik and one Kyrgyz territory in the part that is Uzbek. I hope that's clear but perhaps a Venn diagram is needed to explain such a complex issue! The enclaves may appear as lines on a map but that belies the disputed borders and ethnic violence. The reason that the fourteen million population would want to fight for land in the valley is because there is plentiful fertile soil here growing a range of fruit and nuts. The fighting is more common as the land becomes more arid (possibly through global warming) resulting in more population pressure on the land. Villagers have to criss-cross international borders to access water and food markets as the area's complex border patchwork is now nicknamed "the chessboard border". One of the largest enclaves is Sokh which has almost 99% of its population as Tajiks but is surrounded by Kyrgyzstan and is under the sovereign territory of Uzbekistan. A recipe for discord and security problems if ever there was one. You would think that with a name like "Heavenly Mountains" the residents would be able to agree and save the area from turmoil. Unfortunately, the same environmental problem that much of the world faces has an effect here as well (for climate change see conclusion). The mountains have lost 27% of their ice which means that the glaciers have lost, in each year, "as much water as all the people of Switzerland, including industry, get through in six years" (Bonnett 2017).

On the pub question "Stan" theme, there are only two countries in the world that are double land locked, meaning you go through two countries to reach the sea. One is Uzbekistan and the other is Liechtenstein. Of interest may be the question: where is the city in Europe furthest from the open sea? The answer is Uzhhorod, a city located in western Ukraine, at the border with Slovakia and near the border with Hungary. The city is nearly equidistant from the three nearest seas: the Baltic, the Adriatic and the Black Sea (650-690 km) making it the most inland city in Europe.

Not too far away in China, there is a semi-autonomous province called Xinjiang located south east of the Kazakh border. It is home to the native Muslim population called Uighurs (pronounced Wee-guhr) and who speak a language related to Turkish. The province borders eight countries: Kyrgyzstan, Russia, Mongolia, Afghanistan, Kazakhstan, India, Pakistan and Tajikistan (Bonnett 2017). Perhaps, having five "Stans" for neighbours there was always going to be trouble here. The Uighurs have tried to declare independence for the state of East Turkestan, especially in 2009 when there was inter-ethnic rioting. Unfortunately, this independence movement did not have a lot in its favour. Not only did this region border eight other countries so protecting the heartland of China, but it also has large reserves of oil and is also where the Chinese nuclear testing sites are located. Independence is also unlikely because it is an integral part of Chinese economic strategy of "One Belt, One Road" (OBOR). The project is often described as a 21st century silk road, made up of a "belt" of overland corridors and a maritime "road" of shipping lanes. Some call it the Chinese Marshall Plan (named after the US Secretary of State's rebuilding plan after the 2nd World War) as it is a scheme for Chinese investment and the building of infrastructure around the world. The economic investment in this strategy by the Chinese is estimated to be about £760 billion, give or take a few billion pounds. Unfortunately, the route goes straight through Xinjiang (the Uighurs' home province) connecting southwards to a deep-water port that China is building in Gwadar, Pakistan. China has a forty-year lease on the port thereby connecting the belt and the road. An enclave or any land for the beleaguered Uighur community seems to be as far away as ever.

In Europe, Moldova is a land-locked country located between Ukraine and Romania, which broke away from the Soviet Union in 1991. It has a total population of about 3.5 million with several different nationalities. Perhaps you have not heard anyone talk about Moldova, possibly because it is the least visited country in Europe and people have claimed that it is also the poorest country in Europe. When you think of large volume wine producing nations you would probably think of France or Australia and may be surprised to read that Moldova is the 22nd largest producer of wine in the world (a throwback to when it produced wine for much of the USSR). If more people knew that wine-producing fact, it would certainly become a more visited country. One of the poorest areas within Moldova is the province of Gagauzia. Culturally, the Gagauz people are more Russian-oriented than the rest of the Moldovans. There has been a growing independence movement resulting in the raising of a flag (a dramatic red wolf's head on a white circle) and a government installed in their capital called Kormat. A referendum was held in 1994 which resulted in a patchwork of four unevenly sized enclaves across Moldova. Each of these enclaves contain about 160,000 people spread out over an area of about 707 square miles (1830 square kilometres).

Moldova must have an affection for enclaves because there is another enclave in the country called Transnistria, meaning beyond the river Dniester. It is unrecognised as a nation by any member of the United Nations despite declaring its independence in 1990, a year before the Soviet Union disintegrated. Transnistria is a curious place and remarkably only seventy kilometres south-east of the Moldovan capital of Chisinau. Transnistria's capital called Tiraspol is often described as being stuck in the USSR: with Lenin statues and roads named after Soviet leaders such as Khrushchev. There are three states in the world that recognise Transnistria: Abkhazia, Nagorno-Karabakh, and South Ossetia who are all, incidentally, disputed territories themselves. It has its own constitution, government, passports, currency and military. Essentially, the passport is a useless document for its approximately 500,000 residents because it is not a recognised document. However, they are not trapped in this enclave as most residents hold dual or triple nationality with Russia, Moldova or Ukraine. In 2019 the spectacle of a military parade marking Transnistria's twenty-ninth year of independence illustrated the region's allegiance with Russia. There was much of the old Soviet military hardware such as rockets on display. On the other hand, the military band launched into a rendition of American rock group Survivor's 1982 hit "Eye of the Tiger"! Noticeably, in spite of being an enclave inside Moldova and being bankrolled by Russia, Transnistria still wants to hold on to its independence. It is a curious place, and some say it warrants the title "the place that didn't get the memo that the Cold War was over" (Reid 2020). Transnistria as well as South Ossetia, Artsakh, and Abkhazia are sometimes referred to as post-Soviet "frozen conflict" zones which are disputed territorial areas (always useful for questions in pub or Zoom quizzes).

South Ossetia and Abkhazia are disputed territories in the Caucasus region. The central government of Georgia considers the republics to be under military occupation of Russia after the twelve-day de facto war in 2008. Sara Pascoe in her excellent programme "Last Woman on Earth" (Pascoe 2021) visited the illegal border which was patrolled by vigilantes. There were fifteen volunteers stopping Russian incursions and them moving the border forward. Sara interviewed people who woke up overnight on the wrong side of the border cut off from Georgia. In effect people became stateless overnight.

"Going around the bend" is an expression that is often aimed at me, possibly for obvious reasons. The expression comes from the port city of Khasab where British telegraph officers were stationed in searing heat on a remote rocky outcrop. As they were desperate to return to civilisation, just around the bend of the promontory or rocky outcrop, the expression was born. The location lies on the Musandam peninsula which is a Governorate, or exclave, separated from the rest of Oman by the UAE, in the Middle East. Access to the peninsula was previously difficult and the only options were limited flights or a ten-hour drive through four immigration posts! Also, there is a town called Madha which is an exclave of Oman. Inside this town is a second-order enclave called Nahwa which is part of the UAE. Madha is part of the Musandam Governate and is on the Fujjairah-Khor Fakkan road in the emirate of Sharjah belonging to the UAE. It is the only territory between the UAE and Oman that is not lined with any barrier and there is no border crossing between Madha, Nahwa or the UAE. It reflects a different although mystifying story of borders. In this part of the Middle East, until recently, borders were not necessarily fixed and tribal groups were the most important social and political structure. Large parts of Arabia did not have a Westphalian system until recently (named after the Peace of Westphalia in 1648 which ended the Thirty Years' War among the Catholic and Protestant states in central Europe). It is a global system based on the principle of international law that each state has sovereignity over its territory and domestic affairs. Some people believe that the colonial history, and in particular the Sykes-Picot line from 1916, has a large part to play in the unrest in this region (see chapter seven).

An exclave can have either limited or full sovereign rights of its territory. An example of full rights would be a triangular piece of land in Syria that belongs to Turkey. It is regarded as vital land to Turkey as it contains the Tomb (mausoleum) of Suleyman Shah. He was the grandfather of Osman I, the founder of the Ottoman Empire (nothing to do with Richard Osman the author and host of the popular television quiz show *Pointless*). The tomb has been moved several times, firstly because it was threatened with flooding from the formation of the people-made Lake Assad. In 2015, as a result of the Syrian civil war, it was transferred to a site only 180 metres from the Syrian border and guarded by forty Turkish soldiers. This situation is said to be a temporary arrangement, so the tomb may well have to be moved yet again.

In Europe, Christiania, also known as Freetown Christiania, is a commune covering 7.7 hectares (19 acres) in the borough of Christianshavn within the crowded Danish capital city of Copenhagen. Its creation took place when squatters moved into a military area in 1971. The spirit of Christiania quickly developed into one of the hippie movement, the squatter movement, collectivism, and anarchism which contrasted markedly with the site's previous military use. The people in Christiania have developed their own set of rules, independent of the Danish government, for example its well-known cannabis trade was tolerated by the authorities until 2004. Christiania's housing area is full, with 850 to 1000 residents, so no one can move in without the agreement of one of the autonomous "villages" based on a "one in, one out" system. The message proclaimed from this enclave is "no borders, no nations" and yet in order for the residents of Christiania to be free, paradoxically other people are not free to join them (Bonnett 2017).

Andorra is the sixth smallest nation in Europe (only covering a total of 453 square kilometres/175 square miles), located on the French-Spanish border often called "the country in the mountains". It is an autonomous co-principality under the joint sovereignty of the Bishop of Urgel in Spain and the French Chief of State. What this means is that the President of France is effectively the Prince of Andorra. Many tourists want to visit Andorra visualising a spiritual and cultural mountain kingdom which is a getaway from the pressures of life. However, the zig-zag road climbing up into the Pyrenees leads to a busy duty-free shopping centre swarming with other tourists buying meretricious souvenirs, electrical goods, alcohol, tobacco and designer clothes. Hardly an escape from the tourist crowds of Europe. The main, and possibly only, cultural attraction is the National Museum of Automobiles, notable for its unique collection of 141 different types of spark plugs. Unmissable! The thought of all those spark plugs would surely get you started in the morning. Apparently, Andorra has 198 kilometres of tarmac road (three fewer kilometres than it has ski runs) and a total of 38,201 registered cars and lorries. So, if every Andorran was to drive on the road at the same time, there would be one vehicle for every 5.18 metres of tarmac: basically, a nose to tail traffic jam throughout the entire principality (Crane 1996). Its football team has a special place in the hearts of the English, because they were the first team to play England at the new Wembley stadium, which bizarrely would comfortably accommodate the entire 70,000 population of Andorra!

Remaining in Europe, an Irish penniless and unpublished writer arrived in Trieste in 1904. He was James Joyce who wrote two classic books "Portrait of the Artist as a Young Man" and "Ulysses". I wanted to see his statue over the Canal Grande in this part of Italy which was not overrun with tourists like Venice. Joyce called Trieste "Europiccola" meaning it was like a miniature Europe. Jan Morris called it "a loitering kind of place"; I agreed as it has such a wonderful character as you wander into the piazza squares open on one side to the stunning Adriatic Sea. The marvellous swimming pool and sand lido called Piscina Agonistica is wonderfully old fashioned and tends to be frequented by Triestines rather than tourists. You can listen to local people around the cafe area sitting in the sea water or at the bar drinking Italian coffee or a traditional aperitivo. Jan Morris also describes the city as "an enclave sui generis" meaning in a class by itself, because it is unlike any other Italian city and only five miles from the Slovenian border (Morris 2001). Trieste has changed ownership several times in its 2,000-year history. It's been an Austrian-Habsburg port, the site of a Napoleonic occupation and, briefly, an independent city-state. After the second world war, it was Churchill's southern outpost of the "Iron Curtain" dividing the West from the communist East (see chapter one). Immediately after World War Two, Trieste, on the border with Yugoslavia, was recognised as a free state under international law, though it remained under military occupation until 1954 when it was returned to Italy. The members of the Free Territory of Trieste Movement cite a 1947 United Nations Security Council charter. It recognised Trieste and its surroundings, including parts of what are now Croatia and Slovenia, as a free state with both Italian and Slovenian as official languages. Some people in the Movement want the city to develop into a type of "Adriatic Singapore" which would appear to be unlikely as it is a member of the EU. One of my purposes for visiting Trieste was to cross the border into Slovenia via the hybrid funicular tramway which travelled from the city centre to Opicina, rising over 325 metres into the hills. A fun way to cross the border to the green and picturesque capital city of Ljubjiana and scenic Lake Bled - or so I thought until there was a bad accident in August 2016, and the line was closed and replaced by a much less romantic service, a diesel bus which is much less scenic (Morris 2011).

As Trieste is no longer an exclave of Italy, it leaves Campione d'Italia as the country's only exclave. It is located twenty-three kilometres within Switzerland on the banks of Lake Lugano. With fewer than 2,000 residents, the exclave results from a territorial adjustment in the 16th century. Visitors coming from Switzerland observe a grandiose arch marking the frontier and yet Campione appears to be just another part of Switzerland. Campione's residents drive with Swiss number plates, have their water purified and their rubbish collected by Swiss utility companies. Their telephones are supplied by Swisscom and their purchases are exempt from VAT. It was, in effect, in the Swiss customs area with shopping done mainly in Swiss francs. The main source of income for Italy's exclave was its casino founded in 1917, the largest in Europe and owned by the local government. When the casino closed in 2018 the exclave struggled financially. Many people believed that this strange modernistic cubic-shaped, ochre-coloured building should have been closed and pulled down years ago. In January 2020, Campione d'Italia was brought into the EU customs area, resulting in the need for new duties and checks with even the possibility, dare I write it, of a border-crossing to be established!

If Campione d'Italia is Italy's only exclave, Seborga may be classed as its only enclave. The small hilltop town in north western Italy was designated a principality of the Holy Roman Empire, remaining independent for six hundred years. It was sold to the House of Savoy in 1729 in a transaction that was not registered. Even after the abdication of the Savoy king in 1946 and Italy became a republic, Seborga is not mentioned. In 1995 a referendum confirmed its independence and the head of the local flower-growers cooperative accepted the title of His Tremendousness, driving a black Mercedes with a registration plate number 0001 (Middleton 2011). Although he passed away in 2009, Seborga is still looking to be recognised by Italy as an independent state. How tremendous that would be!

Also, in this part of Europe, on 1st August every year, Switzerland's National Day is celebrated with the familiar flag of a white cross in the centre of a red square background, flying in the town of Büsingen am Hochrhein. It is a perfect holiday scene, except that these celebrations marking the anniversary of

Switzerland's confederation take place in Germany! Surrounded by Switzerland, but owned by Germany, Büsingen am Hochrhein has managed a binational existence for centuries. Technically, it is both an exclave and an enclave. The town has German laws and a German government although it still has the Swiss economy. This absurdity goes back to 1918, after the First World War, when a referendum was held in Büsingen in which 96% of eligible residents voted to become part of Switzerland. However, no land transfer took place as Switzerland could not offer anything suitable in exchange. Later attempts to transfer the village to Swiss sovereignty were unsuccessful and consequently Büsingen has remained an exclave of Germany ever since. Büsingen officially entered into a customs union with Switzerland in 1967, although the town is still classed as part of Germany. There is an intriguing tourist path, which Büsingen interchangeably calls the "Enclave or Exclave Trail", taking in river views, international border markers and even a vineyard, where terraces of German Riesling and Pinot Noir grapes ripen before they're transported in lorries a few kilometres - to be made into Swiss wine! The trail's first stop, a town hall mural on Büsingen's main street, illustrates the dichotomy here, because there is a painting of a smiling worker holding a pole flying a German flag; another one shows a Swiss worker with a Swiss flagpole sticking out of his jacket pocket. The town division is as evident as Baarle-Hertog (see chapter three), illustrated by the Restaurant Waldheim. A line painted across its outdoor dining terrace marks the international border, so it's possible to be served a stein of pilsner beer in Germany and on the other side of the table a plate of raclette cheese in Switzerland (Bleiberg 2013).

Rome is a wonderful city for a walking visit as you can enter the Colosseum, wander up the Spanish Steps and pose by or throw coins into the waters of the Trevi fountain, all in a single day. Walking down fashionable Via Condotti I spotted the Magisterial Palace at number 68, which belongs to the smallest sovereign country in the world consisting of only 6,000 square metres: The Sovereign Military Order of Malta. It is over a thousand years old and is formally recognised in international organisations and acknowledged for its medical, humanitarian and social projects that take place in over 120 countries. Geopolitically odd, its aims are the defence of the (Catholic) faith and assistance to the poor. However, it is a state without a territory and a sovereignty without borders. It has a small passport office, in fact very small, mainly because there are only two passports issued so they are the most exclusive in the world (although there are 400 diplomatic passports as well). Despite having a population of only two (a prince and a grand master) and being the smallest country in the world, you can argue that its influence reaches everywhere. It is recognised by about 106 countries (although significantly not China, USA and India), maintains dozens of embassies, has a permanent observer to the UN and is represented at the World Health Organisation. Unusually, The Sovereign Military Order of Malta used to have its own air force and curiously an army run as a medical unit in the Italian armed forces maintaining its own hospital train with 192 beds. It did have territory on the Greek island of Rhodes (not to be confused with the state in the USA), in Malta (no surprise considering its name) and on four Caribbean islands (Bonnett 2017). Undoubtedly, many large and emerging countries would be jealous of the recognition that The Sovereign Military Order of Malta receives even though it can still be classed as the smallest country in the world.

I travelled south from north Italy into Croatia, staying at the enchanting port of Split. I wanted to visit as much of Croatia's rocky coastline in a year as possible before reaching the former capital known as Dubrovnik. Unusually, it is not possible (as yet) to drive along this limestone coastline to its former capital because Dubrovnik is an exclave of Croatia. When Yugoslavia was a communist country, its leader Marshal Tito decided to award the republic of Bosnia-Herzegovina a symbolic outlet to the sea at Neum, even though this road would travel through Croatia. The lines that he drew on a map for administrative convenience have now an international border. The border crossing at Neum means that it is impossible to drive from Split to Dubrovnik without passing through Bosnia-Herzegovina which is not in the EU (Croatia is in the EU). So, you have to drive from Croatia to Bosnia and back into Croatia all within six miles, showing your passports each time - a time-consuming drive especially in the height of the hot summer tourist season. Anxious to create a single stretch of continuous territory so that Dubrovnik is more accessible, Croatia has begun work on an expensive bridge. It runs to the Peljesac peninsular, linking the two cities of Split and Dubrovnik, bypassing Neum. Of course, if Bosnia joins the EU, many believe that this bridge, that will cost 420 million euros, will have been a white elephant because there would be no hard border anyway (see Schengen agreement chapter one).

Who do you name your local airport after? An easy task if you live in Liverpool - John Lennon, and if you live in New Orleans - Louis Armstrong. The naming of Doncaster airport was difficult, although calling it Robin Hood airport has the imagination of a non-geographer (because it is nowhere near Sherwood Forest). Immanuel Kant lived in the Russian exclave of Kaliningrad nestled between Poland and Lithuania, about the size of Northern Ireland, 330 kilometres from Moscow. Kaliningrad was part of Germany until it was annexed by Russia after World War II. The philosopher Immanuel Kant spent all his life in the city philosophising that there was no need to venture abroad. He believed that ships came and brought people so that they could tell him lots of meaningful stories. Undoubtedly, Kant was not into the philosophy of travel, dying there in 1804, having never left the city. There has been a campaign to name the local airport Kant airport, after this great German thinker. Russian locals left flyers (no pun intended) around his monument and painted it pink, proclaiming that "the name of the German Kant will not tarnish our airport." There was a need for careful pronunciation, after all it's only an airport name! Kaliningrad has a huge, ugly white building near the city centre that can be best described as a "monstrosity". The Dom Sovietov or The House of Soviets (even I can work that one out in Russian) was constructed on top of the ruins of the Königsberg Castle, known to locals as "The Monster" or "The Robot's Head". Not only does it look like a poorly planned piece of architecture, it was deemed structurally unsound and therefore has never been occupied. Rumour has it that a mysterious owner prevents it from being demolished.

Another place to visit in Kaliningrad is the cathedral in front of which has been placed a statue of Lenin. It is not clear whether it was accidentally or deliberately located here, because he was a strong proponent of atheism. This city has always been an important place for the high ranking officials from Moscow, especially as it is the birthplace of Lyudmila Ocheretnaya, a former flight attendant for the Kaliningrad branch of Aeroflot. She is better known as Mrs Putin (now ex Mrs Putin). Kaliningrad is very important to Russia because it is the country's only port that stays ice-free throughout the year, so it has been heavily militarised. It houses the Russian Baltic Fleet at the port of Baltiysk and is one of the most secretive and inaccessible areas of Russia and probably the world. Allegedly, the Kaliningrad "oblast" (region) harbours the largest concentration of military equipment in Europe. The area was part of Germany until annexation by the USSR following World War II when it saw bitter fighting and suffered extensive destruction. The German population was expelled or fled after the war ended. During the Soviet period, Kaliningrad was re-built on a grandiose scale with plentiful statues representing Lenin, Stalin, Kalinin and Pushkin – I suppose that you had to be part of the "in" crowd to have a statue dedicated in your name. Although administratively part of the Russian Federation, it was separated from the rest of Russia, by the then Soviet republics of Lithuania, Latvia and Belarus. High-ranking generals and members of the Politburo could head off here to enjoy the glorious beaches of the Baltic sea. However, since Lithuania joined the EU in 2004, it has been impossible to travel over land between the Kaliningrad exclave and the rest of Russia without crossing the territory of at least one EU state. There has been resistance and friction, particularly with neighbouring Lithuania, over border and access regulations. Kant would not have wanted trouble in his place of birth as he stated "all immoral actions are irrational"; therefore, he may not have been too disappointed about not achieving his own named airport.

Exclaves and enclaves exist on the North American continent as well (see quirky borders in chapter six). There is a barrier that divides TMR (Town of Mount Royal, a model suburb developed as a largely upper income community in the 1950s and 1960s) and Park Extension, the low income, largely immigrant neighbourhood immediately to the east of TMR on the island of Montreal. It is obvious for whom the barrier has been constructed. As Basil Fawlty would say in the television comedy programme *Fawlty Towers*, it was built to "keep the riff-raff out". The area forms an enclave in the centre of Montreal. The L'Acadie Wall hems it in on the west, railways border the neighbourhood on the east and south with Highway 40 forming the northern boundary. The four borders make Parc Extension an enclave creating a crowded community with 33,000 people in an area 1.5 square kilometres. Gisele Amantea who has photographed this barrier calls it "clôture de la honte" meaning the fence of shame. Ironically, there is a relic of the Berlin wall in Montreal which was a gift to the city, perhaps a symbol of hope that barriers such as this can be torn down (Di Cintio 2012).

Neither an exclave or an enclave, a panhandle or salient is a piece of land extending away from the host country. There may be many places in the world that one legitimately can call "the roof of the world" but the Wakhan Corridor (panhandle) is one of the best candidates: located in the far north east corner of the country, and surrounded on three sides by Tajikistan, Pakistan and China. Remarkably, the Wakhan is cut off from the rest of Afghanistan. There are no government services, large parts of the region have no roads and people are basically living in their own small groups in the mountains. Crossing the border is a fairly simple affair by all accounts with limited border control, mainly because the number of tourists that enter Afghanistan is about a 100 - that's per year! The

Wakhan Corridor is part of a 350-kilometre (218 mile) corridor that leads away from Afghanistan so it can have a border with China.

A country that has two panhandles is the Democratic Republic of Congo (DRC), the former Belgium colony in Africa. In my geography lessons, I would call this country a developing country. In reality, it is inaccurate to say it is developing partly because of how the country was put together (see Berlin Conference chapter four). The DRC is struggling economically because it is neither democratic nor a republic, having a population larger than the UK (84 million), and contains over 250 ethnic groups. Arguably, it has the most unreported war zone in the world with six million deaths since the late 1990s. One panhandle is the Congo Central Corridor which extends to link the country to the sea. There is also a 200-kilometre corridor that is still in existence called the Congo Pedicle which cuts into Zambia. The word comes from the Latin "pediculus" meaning little foot; moreover, it is still known today as the Katanga boot. The history suggests that Britain (its colony was Zambia) and Belgium (its colony was Congo, which incidentally was 80 times the size of its Belgium motherland) could not agree on a border, so they got the King of Italy to draw the border. Unfortunately, he had never been to Africa but somehow still produced the border lines! When you look at the Katanga boot extremity on a map, I wish I had noticed it as a schoolchild, because it looks rather rude creating lots more opportunities to embarrass the geography teacher.

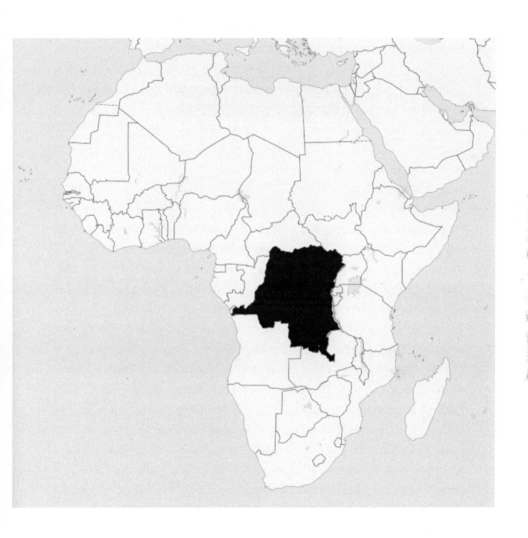

Congo panhandle (Wikimedia)

CHAPTER 6
QUIRKY BORDERS

A good walk spoiled is how I would describe many of my attempts at a round of golf, but not if I went to the northern end of the Gulf of Bothnia near Haparanda. Tornio golf course has a standard eighteen holes but what makes it unusual is that the course runs through two countries and two time zones. It is, perhaps, a unique golf course with nine holes in one country, Finland, and the remaining nine holes in another, Sweden. The border between the two countries follows the Tornio River, which runs through the middle of the course. This golf course might have its professional shop in Finland, but half of the course is in Sweden! It usually takes me five holes to ease and loosen my back and relax into my swing ready for the sixth hole. Here, players tee off in Sweden and the green is in Finland, so with the one-hour time difference, this could be the record for the longest time to complete a par three hole in the world. Also, due to its location and the midnight sun, it is possible to play golf at any time of the day or night in full light during the summer golfing season.

Towns are twinned with some unlikely partners: Coventry and Dresden; Birmingham and Milan; and, my favourite, Dull (Scotland) and Boring (Oregon). There are several twin towns that are in a state of flux, mainly because they do not know which country they belong to. Almost two hundred enclaves called 'chitmahals' are nestled on the India-Bangladesh border. The name is from the Hindi words 'chit', meaning note and 'mahal', meaning palace. They are often referred to by their Indian regional name of Cooch-Behar. It is a series of enclaves not unlike the Baarle-Hertog area in Belgium. Cooch-Behar has the distinction of containing the world's only third-order enclave: an Indian enclave in a Bangladeshi enclave, which is itself in an Indian enclave within Bangladesh - try explaining that after a glass of Kingfisher beer. To clarify this complex situation, this Indo-Bangladeshi border contains over 170 intricately crenelated pockets of territory. There are 102 parcels of India surrounded by Bangladesh and 71 parcels of Bangladesh surrounded by India. More than 50,000 people live in these hilly geopolitical islands, many deprived of basic services because miles of foreign territory separate them from their sovereign country. It may be a myth that the land was won and lost in a game of chess between the Maharajah of Cooch-Behar and the Nawab of Rangpur. Another legend suggests that in 1946 there was a British cartographer who knocked over his inkpot while drawing India's borders. In the morning, the ink blotches had dried to form the most absurd geopolitical map of borders. One suspects that there is little truth in either story, but the chitmahals do represent a weird but international problem. An example is the case of a resident in a Bangladeshi enclave inside India who needed medical treatment. She travelled to the hospital nearest to her chitmahal but, because she was not an Indian citizen, the doctors refused to treat her. Next time she went to the hospital she was in labour, so she hired, and had to pay for, an Indian 'husband' so that her child could be delivered inside the hospital (Sidhwa 1988).

Every February, France hands over 6,820 square metres of its territory to Spain without a single shot being fired. However, six months later, Spain voluntarily handed back the land to France. Pheasant Island (in French Ile des Faisans, in Spanish Isla de los Faisanes) which lies between Spain and France, is not a tourist destination like Mont St Michel and it is uninhabited. It is a tiny islet just over 200 metres long and 40 metres wide that bisects the River Bidasoa. Every year Pheasant Island spends six months under French control, before being handed over to Spain for six months. The reason for such an absurd situation is a complex historical agreement. In 1659, the Spanish and French negotiated the end to their long war on the island, as it was considered neutral territory. Wooden bridges were extended from both sides and the armies stood ready as the negotiations began. A peace agreement was signed called the Treaty of the Pyrenees (it must have been a high-level agreement). Territory was swapped and the border demarcated, and control agreed for half of the year for each country. The deal was sealed with a romantic royal wedding, as the French King Louis XIV married the daughter of the Spanish King Philip IV. Whether they had to live in France for six months and then Spain for six months is not clear. Obviously, this sort of joint sovereignty is rare and it is called a condominium, with Pheasant Island as one of the oldest examples in the world. If the happy couple were looking for a location for a picnic equally as absurd as Pheasant Island the border between Slovakia, Austria and Hungary would have been a fitting locality as it is such a calm place. Tourists can stop at this tripoint and have a truly international meal. There is a three-cornered picnic table where each of the three edges represents the border of each country!

There is a common expression "take one day at a time"; strangely, there are places on earth where you can take two days at a time. The Diomede Islands lie halfway across the Bering Straits, bisecting Alaska and Siberia. In Russia, they are known as the Gvozdev Islands, and consist of two rocky, flat-topped and hilly islands. The two Diomede Islands are separated by the International Date Line. This means that when the residents of Little Diomede, owned by the USA, look across the channel at Big Diomede, owned by Russia, they are looking 21 hours (only 20 hours in the summer) into the future. As a result, the islands are sometimes called Tomorrow Island (Big Diomede) and Yesterday

Island (Little Diomede). So, in theory, you could have two days in twenty-four hours; also you could celebrate two birthdays simply by crossing the International Date Line!

The Aleutian Islands have the distinction that they are the only part of the United States of America that were invaded during World War II. This invasion consisted of the Japanese landings and occupations of Kiska and Attu in June 1942. So that it does not cross nation states, the International Date Line passes around the far east of Russia and other archipelagos in the Pacific. In the north, the date line turns to the east through the Bering Strait and then west past the Aleutian Islands in order to keep Alaska and Russia on opposite sides of the line. This border is so quirky that Alaska has the honour of being the most western, most eastern and most northern state of the USA (Monmonier 1996).

The countries of Lithuania and Belarus both used to be part of the Soviet Union. The paths they went down have been very different after leaving the Union over thirty years ago. Lithuania joined the EU and NATO, whereas Belarus has tended to have affinity with the east and Russia. Shortly after crossing the Lithuanian border, a red flag marks the entrance to the Isyvenimo Drama (translates literally as Survival Drama) an attraction billed as "Europe's Strangest Theme Park". A turning into the forest leads to a vast underground Soviet bunker built in the 1980s to accommodate the Soviet-Lithuanian television corporation in case of a nuclear war. Visitors pay large sums of money, and hand over their cameras and phones, to be humiliated, interrogated, forced to sign false confessions, shown propaganda and taught how to prepare for an attack by the imperialist pigs - that's us in the West by the way (Davies 2012). The tourists, I use that term loosely, get the chance to wear gas masks, eat typical Soviet food and undergo a Soviet medical check. The aim is to make people feel what the Soviet Union was really like. Like any good visitor attraction, there is a treat at the end - you get the chance to drink a shot of authentic Russian vodka.

Colonial powers at The Berlin Conference in 1885 far from settled the permanent borders in Africa (see chapter four). There are many unrecognised countries, twenty-one in fact, represented by the Federation of the Free States of Africa. It is an alliance of sovereign African states, whose aims and purpose are to promote democracy, freedom and peace in Africa. The Federation is also known as the African League for Peace and Prosperity. Members include such dramatic names, even if frustrating for the residents, such as Equateur, Kongo, Lunda Tchokwe and my favourite N'Dongo. These countries are all tied together by the fact that their struggle is largely ignored by the rest of the world. Incidentally, the West African kingdom of Kongo is spelt correctly, and is located within three present-day countries: northern Angola, the western part of the Democratic Republic of the Congo, as well as the southernmost part of Gabon. These nascent countries are taken seriously by the governments whose territory they claim as trouble can often flare-up. The Lunda and the Tchokwe are two related Bantu tribes and the traditional Tchokwe kingdom was conquered by Portugal around 1920. Lunda Tchokwe covers an area almost the size of Spain, is home to over 4.5 million people and contains some of the world's largest diamond mines. With the presence of these valuable mines, it is no wonder that the government of Angola has criminalised the activities of the separatists and forced many activists into exile. The nationalists see the boundaries of Africa based on colonialism and view the African states as the new colonial powers following this system: put simply, they regard them as an extension of European colonialism.

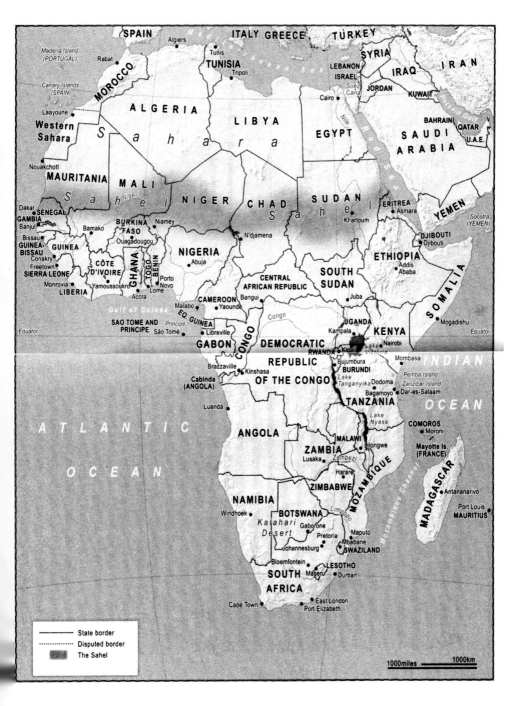

Illustration of a map of Africa (JP Map graphics Ltd)
Swaziland is called Eswatini since 2018

The word territory conjures up images of people wanting to own land, occupy land and even fight for land. Unbelievably, this not always the case. There is an 800 square mile (2060 square kilometre) cartographical oddity of rocky desert that you could claim because nobody wants it. Bir Tawil (meaning tall well) is wedged between Egypt and Sudan and the point of not wanting this land-locked region is that it boasts a claim to a much more useful area of land, called the Hala'ib Triangle, which faces the Red Sea. The dispute arises from two different versions of the border drawn up by British administrators. The first version from 1899, preferred by Egypt, is a straight line of 770 miles (1,240 kilometres) across the desert, giving Bir Tawil to Sudan and Hala'ib Triangle to Egypt. The Sudanese preference is for the 1902 version where the Wadi Halfa Salient along the Nile and Hala'ib Triangle are given to Sudan. Egypt appears to have had its way by disclaiming Bir Tawil, which has become even more unwanted because of a severe drought in the area. Luckily for me I have three wonderful daughters, and it is always difficult for me to find meaningful birthday presents for them - perhaps naming a star in the sky or claiming a piece of land would be the unique present. However, in June 2014, a 38-year-old farmer from Virginia named Jeremiah Heaton beat me to it. After obtaining the necessary paperwork from the Egyptian military authorities, he planted a flag into the no-man's land of Bir Tawil. His six-year-old daughter, Emily, had once asked her father if she could ever be a real princess; after discovering the existence of Bir Tawil on the internet, his birthday present to her that year was to trek on a fourteen-hour expedition to this previously unclaimed territory and turn her wish into a reality. "So be it proclaimed," Heaton wrote on his Facebook page, "that Bir Tawil shall be forever known as the Kingdom of North Sudan. The Kingdom is established as a sovereign monarchy with myself [sic] as the head of state; with Emily becoming an actual princess." Heaton knew his actions would provoke scorn and confusion and many questioned his sanity. There was an angry backlash because he was not seen as a heroic pioneer or someone with a strange sense of humour but rather as a 21st-century imperialist (Bonnett 2014). Some argued that his action legitimised European colonialism not just in Africa but in the Americas, Australia, and elsewhere. "Are white people still allowed to do this kind of stuff?" was one exclamation. After all, the portrayal of land as "unclaimed" or "undeveloped" was central to centuries of ruthless conquest by Europeans. On the other hand, can he be regarded as just a devoted father trying to claim the last truly "unclaimed" land on earth for his daughter? Perhaps selling the film rights to the Disney Corporation, for an undisclosed fee, may give some indication as to the answer to that conundrum (Shenker 2016).

The desire for your own land territory is, perhaps, superseded by a need to have your own island where your borders are physical and beyond doubt. It is difficult to find unclaimed islands so perhaps an abandoned gun platform from the Second World War would suffice. The Principality of Sealand is such a platform, six miles off the Essex coast, not much larger than a tennis court, claimed in 1967 as sovereign territory by a retired army major, 'Paddy' Roy Bates and his wife, Joan. With the titles, prince and princess, they started to develop the rig into a home and kingdom. Sealand's sleeping quarters were hidden inside its windowless, cylindrical legs, with most of the rooms below the waterline. There have been other platform states, such as the bamboo-platform republic of New Atlantis off the west coast of Jamaica, whose president was Leicester, Ernest Hemingway's brother. In 1968, the British navy sent gunboats to remove Bates and he was arrested after firing shots across an approaching boat. He won a court battle by arguing that the platform was outside British national jurisdiction. As a result, the Principality issued gold and silver coins (called the Sealand dollar), passports and stamps. In 1978, Alexander Achenbach, who described himself as prime minister of Sealand, disagreed with Bates over plans to turn Sealand into a luxury hotel and casino. While Bates and his wife were in Austria, Achenbach organised Dutch and German mercenaries to storm the platform with speedboats and helicopters. They took Bate's son, Michael, hostage. In true James Bond style, Michael managed to retake the platform using weapons stored on the platform, capturing Achenbach and the mercenaries. Achenbach, who held a Sealand passport, was charged with treason against Sealand. Quirkily, in 1987 when the UK extended its territorial waters from three to twelve miles, so did Sealand, thereby declaring the annexation of Harwich and Felixstowe on mainland Britain! Bizarrely, when Gianni Versace's killer committed suicide on a Miami houseboat in 1997, he was found to have a Sealand passport, which led to a drugs gang - you've guessed it, they all had Sealand passports as well! By not concentrating on these legal entanglements, one can concentrate on the charming life that an island (or even a platform) can provide, as Princess Joan Bates summarised in the Sealand Newspaper:

"It's been a fairy tale. What greater compliment can a man pay to a woman than to make her a princess of her own Principality? I love being able to call myself Princess. When we travel abroad on our Sealand passports, we are always greeted with a lot of fuss and treated like royalty".

The lure of independence and sovereignty can be a very appealing fantasy (MacEacheran 2020).

The water around Sealand and the British Isles is reassuringly observed by Radio 4 broadcasting the shipping forecast four times a day. Some people regard it as the most British thing ever, even quirkier than cricket. The charm of the forecast is not only its eye-catching names, such as Fitzroy (who founded the Meteorological Office) or Trafalgar (only mentioned in the fourth forecast of the day), but also because the apparently random borders are simply straight lines. Charlie Connelly wrote a hilarious account (yes, honestly) in his book bestseller The Shipping Forecast (Connelly 2004)). He described areas such as sandbanks called Fisher or Dogger (from the Dutch word "dogge" and meaning fishing boat). I recall my hilarious lesson when trying to teach the book Kes (A Kestrel for a Knave by Barry Hines) to pubescent Australian students when they had no idea what a Barnsley accent sounded like or what Fisher and German Bight meant when the register was taken (Hines 1968). My favourite story of the shipping forecast borders relates to Marilyn Monroe. Utsire is a tiny island about fifteen miles off Haugesund, and it is the only area that has two shipping forecast areas named after it (North and South Utsire). There was a resident of Haugesund who immigrated to the USA in the 1920s. He had a daughter called Norma Jean, so this town has become an important link to Marilyn Monroe fans. The town erected a statue of her in her memory even though the association is somewhat tenuous and has been subject to much argument.

Another name in the shipping forecast is Rockall, which is an isolated, uninhabited granite islet in the North Atlantic Ocean. It was claimed by the UK in 1955 (there is a plaque on the island that says so), making it the last territorial expansion of the British Empire. It is about 300 kilometres (190 miles) west of the Scottish island of Soay, and 425 kilometres (265 miles) north-west of Tory Island, Ireland. Considering how close it is to the UK, fewer than twenty people have been thought to have ever landed on it, which suggests that more people have landed on the moon than have landed on Rockall! In 1978, eight members of the Dangerous Sports Club held a cocktail party on the island. I am not a member of this club, and, after studying their annual party venues, I am unlikely to become one. In 1997, the environmentalist organisation Greenpeace occupied the islet calling it Waveland, not the most imaginative name so far out in the ocean. They were protesting against oil exploration. Greenpeace declared the island to be a "new Global State" as a spoof micronation (see chapter seven) and offered citizenship to anyone willing to take their pledge of allegiance. The British Government's response was to state that "Rockall is British territory. It is part of Scotland and anyone is free to go there". During his one night on Rockall, Greenpeace protester and Guardian journalist John Vidal unscrewed the 1955 plaque and re-fixed it back-to-front (I bet he was the student at school who sat at the back of the classroom throwing paper aeroplanes).

Across the other side of the world, the Trans-Mongolian railway is 6,300 kilometres long (3,915 miles), taking over ten days to cross two continents and five time zones. The railway line crosses from Mongolia to China at the twin towns of Zamyn-Uud and Erenhot. The crossing is a train enthusiast's paradise as the wheels or bogies are changed at the border. Mongolia and China use different gauges of train track, which means all train carriages, with the passengers still on board, need to be lifted up and have one set of wheels removed and a different set fixed. Apparently, different visas are needed for both China and Mongolia and it is also advisable to make a precautionary visit to the lavatory before the bogie-changing, as passengers are locked out of these facilities during the lengthy process.

What happens on the road when a drive-on-the-left country meets a country that drives on the right? Most countries in the world drive on the right, so there is normally not a problem. If the countries do drive on the left, such as Australia, Britain and Japan, they are islands, so the border issue does not really arise. Major exceptions are shown in south-east Africa and the Indian sub-continent, where the countries tend to come grouped together in clusters and mostly border each other. However, there are a few countries that do have to switch traffic lanes at the border crossing. Thailand, which drives on the left, has three of its neighbours, Cambodia, Laos, and Myanmar, that drive on the right. Most of its busiest borders just use a simple traffic light solution to alternate the flow of vehicles. However, there are more intricate solutions allowing for continuous traffic. Macau was a Portuguese colony for more than 400 years and was handed back to China in 1999 as the last European colony in Asia (Hong Kong was handed over from Britain in 1998). Macau still drives on the left under Chinese rule, which means travellers between Macau and other parts of China must switch sides of the road without even leaving the country. At the Lotus Bridge between Macau and Hengqin Island, cars on the

Chinese side loop under the bridge on a "weirdly asymmetric partial cloverleaf" in order to switch lanes (Jennings 2013).

Of course, rather than the Lotus Bridge, China is more famous for The Great Wall of China as one of the most celebrated human building achievements. Built in the 2nd century BC, The Great Wall is more than 2,300 years old. That is one very old monument! The Great Wall snakes its way across Northern China, built by Qin Shi Huangdi (circa 259-210 BC), who was the first emperor of China during the Qin (or Ch'in) dynasty. Throughout history, although the Great Wall wasn't consistently worked on, China's dynasties have added to this structure, which served as a defence mechanism and protection against their enemies. During the Qin Dynasty, construction of the wall was by convicted criminals as part of their sentence. At the time of construction, no machines were available, and construction was all down to manpower. Crimes like tax evasion were punishable by wall construction (it would have been a lucky escape for certain high-profile comedians). Its primary purpose was to protect the Chinese Empire, although there is evidence that nomads came across it, and the invasion past the Great Wall by Manchus, in fact, led to the collapse of the Ming Dynasty. The wall, which is over 21,000 kilometres long (13,000 miles), has been called many different names. I am not sure where the inspiration comes from to call it "The Long Wall"! In China, as a symbol of their culture, it is called "The Earth Dragon". The Great Wall of China is the name most popularly used in the UK and in the USA. Other countries let their imagination run wild and call it "The Chinese Wall"! Natural weathering and human footpath erosion have led to parts of the wall disappearing and according to statistics from UNESCO, nearly one third of the wall has already been destroyed. The wall can be subject to over 10 million visitors per year and approximately 30,000 tourists a day in some locations like Badaling - let's hope they are all walking in the same direction in order to avoid congestion! Most of the Great Wall was constructed by earth, brick, wood, and stones, but staggeringly rice was a key ingredient in holding the Great Wall together. In my kitchen, after boiling rice for too long, I can see the reason why it could be used as a building material. Also known as 'sticky rice', and not only a staple of the Chinese diet, the rice was used as a result of its cohesive properties. By the way, it is a myth that the Great Wall of China can be seen from space by the naked eye - it would be like trying to see a length of hair from two miles away.

It has often astonished me that the continents of North and South America are not named after Christopher Columbus, the Italian explorer who sailed to the area between 1492 and 1504. In fact, the word America comes from a much less famous navigator, another Italian explorer, called Amerigo Vespucci. Like Columbus, Vespucci travelled to the New World (firstly in 1499 and again in 1502). Unlike Columbus, Vespucci wrote down what he knew about this New World. When Vespucci's accounts of his travels were published, they were widely read in Europe. Columbus was also hindered because he thought he had discovered another route to Asia rather than a whole new continent. Vespucci called the new continent the New World, or Novus Mundus in Latin. In 1507, a German cartographer named Martin Waldseemüller drew a map of the world that was approximately 2.4 metres wide and 1.3 metres high with 12 wooden panels. He based his map, called Universal Cosmography, and drawings of the New World on Vespucci's published travelogues. At the time, all countries were named as female nouns, so Waldseemüller used a feminine, Latin form of Amerigo to name the new continent "America." He later realised that he should have called the new continent after Columbus, and he tried to take the name off the map, but cartographers tended to copy one another's choices and the name had stuck. Columbus was left off the map, so we will never have the United States of Columbia, much to the relief of songwriters Paul Simon (who wrote "America") and Don McLean (who wrote "American Pie").

When referring to borders, I should also refer to another one of my favourite musicians, Mark Knopfler, a legend from the superb band Dire Straits. He composed an album and song called "Sailing to Philadelphia". If you ever get the chance to listen to the lyrics, you'll hear that he sings about Jeremiah Dixon, a Geordie (in the first line), and Charlie Mason, who was a baker's boy from the West Country (in the first line of the second verse). You may think that this is irrelevant to borders and the USA. On further investigation, the song's lyrics refer to a pair of surveyors travelling to North America and "sailing to Philadelphia to draw the line – the Mason-Dixon line" (Knopfler 2000). One of these famous men was someone I admired: Mason was a meticulous observer of nature and geography who later became a fellow of the Royal Observatory in Greenwich; Dixon was expelled from the Quakers for his drinking and keeping loose company. The two men had previously come together to map the transit of Venus, thereby making it easier to calculate the earth's distance from the sun. In the 1760s they were sent to settle a border dispute between Maryland and Pennsylvania (now in the USA). They helped to demarcate the line between the two states and its later unofficial extension west along the Ohio River. This line came to symbolise the great divide between the North and the South, between the slave and non-slave states that later fought the American Civil War. For 80 years, the Calvert family from Maryland and the Penn family from Pennsylvania had been locked in a disagreement over the boundary between the two colonies that they had been granted by the English Crown. Outdated maps meant new and correct measurements were needed, but colonial surveyors had produced inaccurate work. The families hired Mason and Dixon, who were known in England as master astronomers and surveyors. Mason and Dixon brought with them some of the most advanced surveying equipment ever seen, including tools by renowned instrument maker John Bird, who, like Dixon, hailed from County Durham. They used Bird's instruments to calculate the path by the stars encountering hostile Native Americans, mountains, dense forest, rivers and wild animals. The Mason-Dixon Line was drawn in two parts. A 133.5 kilometre north-south divide between Maryland and Delaware and the more recognised 375 kilometres west to east divide between Pennsylvania and Maryland, stretching from just south of

Philadelphia to what is now West Virginia. Stones were imported, measuring up to 1.5 metres high and up to 225 kilograms in weight, quarried from oolitic limestone from the Isle of Portland near the English Channel. They were placed every mile and marked with a P for Pennsylvania and M for Maryland on each side of the line. These so-called Crown stones were positioned every five miles and engraved with the Penn family's coat of arms on one side and the Calvert family's signage on the other. The idea of trying to stay on a line of latitude for 230 miles through the wilderness with equipment that had never been used before is incredible (Mawson 2017). Inevitably, there were bound to be some inaccuracies, mainly due to the influence of gravity on the equipment, but their boundary mapping was a staggering achievement.

It is likely that Mason and Dixon never heard of the phrase "Mason–Dixon line" because the survey report did not mention them, and they both died relatively young and in obscurity. Their names remain because it is still a demarcation line between four US states, forming part of the borders of Pennsylvania, Maryland, Delaware, and West Virginia. The Mason-Dixon line came into use during the debate around the Missouri Compromise of 1820, when the boundary between slave (Southern) and free (Northern) states was an issue. It is still used today in the figurative sense of a line that separates the North and South politically and socially. Some proclaim that their achievement was the equivalent of the moon landings - as a matter of fact, Mason did have a moon crater named after him! Some people believe that the term Dixie originates from Jeremiah's surname (Cornwall 2012). Others believe that it is from the French Quarter of the city of New Orleans where the local banks issued ten-dollar notes labelled Dix (French for ten) on the reverse side. However, their legacy lives on despite Mason and Dixon not being famous during their own lifetime.

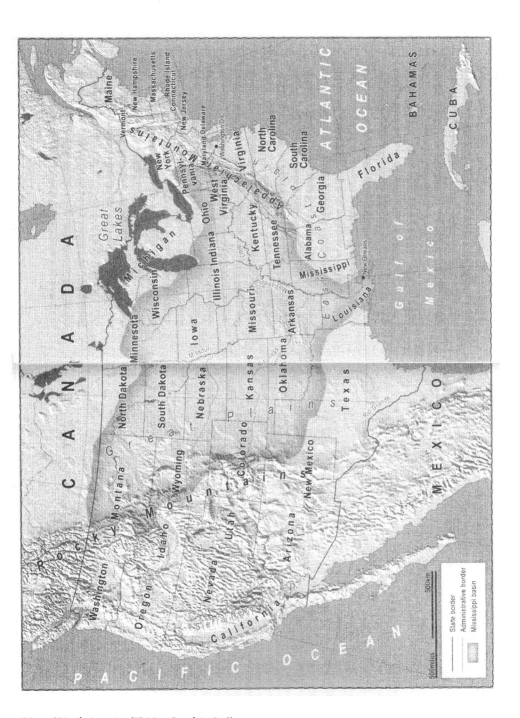

Map of North America (JP Map Graphics Ltd)

In the plot of the famous film "Wizard of Oz", Dorothy and her dog Toto want to return to their home in Kansas. The team, Kansas City Chiefs, win the 2020 Super Bowl final and return to their families to celebrate in their home state. However, most of Kansas City is not actually in the state of Kansas but is mainly in the state of Missouri, with only a much smaller part of the city in the state of Kansas. Taxes tend to be lower on the Missouri side, so most businesses and residents have tended to move there. There is a famous highway called State Line Road, which is about 20 kilometres long (13 miles), that divides the two states and represents one of the most unique borders in the world. You can see eighteen-year-old students crossing this road from Missouri state to Kansas state because the legal limit for drinking alcohol in Missouri is twenty-one years old and only eighteen years old in Kansas!

Every geography teacher, including myself, loves to teach about the landform called an ox-bow lake. For many students it is possibly the only feature they remember from a full year's geography lessons. The fact that is difficult to perceive what one looks like, apart from on aerial or drone photographs, is always irrelevant to the teacher! To recap on this wonderful feature, it is a river landform that is a small freshwater lake located in a cut-off meander loop of a river. I am sure your geography teacher explained, in some detail, that it is named after a U-shaped collar placed around the neck of an ox upon which a plough is attached. The city of Carter Lake is one example of the border irregularities of the United States simply because of this landform. In March 1877, a flood redirected the course of the Missouri river about two kilometres to the south-east. The remnants of the old river's course, called Saratoga Bend, became an ox-bow lake, and was named Carter Lake. This area became popular for residents and was claimed by Iowa even though it was west of the river. In 1930, a court ruling meant that Carter Lake was officially incorporated as a city into the state of Iowa. So, rather confusingly, Carter Lake has become a unique location because it is the only city in the state of Iowa that is located west of the

Missouri River, even though it is a suburb of Omaha, in the state of Nebraska!

Another example of an ox-bow loop defining a border is an island in Kentucky (the Bluegrass State) surrounded by the states of Tennessee and Missouri. On an aerial map, it looks like a "bubble" of Kentucky pushing the Mississippi River in a northerly direction: this is the reason why seventeen square miles of land is known locally as "Bubbleland". In 1811 and 1812, there was a series of large earthquakes that rocked the region of New Madrid near the meeting of the states of Missouri, Tennessee, and Kentucky. The force of the tectonic movement created a meander in the Mississippi River and formed an ox-bow geographical oddity. The border between the states was always defined by the Mississippi River. Where there is no river, the boundary between Tennessee and Kentucky is defined by the 35.5 degrees north parallel line. As surveyors became more accurate, so this line of latitude drifted north; when the line reached the Tennessee River, it was a tenth of a degree out. As a result, the border was extended to the Mississippi river in 1819, on the correct line. The Kentucky Bend, also known as Madrid or Bessie's Bend, only has one road that connects it to Tennessee, so children have to take a 12-mile bus ride to the nearest school in Tiptonville, Tennessee. Today, there are fewer than twenty residents, but if any of them are old enough and need to vote, a forty-mile trip to Hickman is required (Jennings 2019). If they want to watch the Kentucky Derby, they have to drive through Tennessee. This odd border sparked the imagination of none other than Mark Twain, who wrote about a local family feud there in his 1883 memoir *Life on the Mississippi* (Twain 2021). In Twain's version, two Kentucky Bend clans (the Darnell and Watson families) attended the same church at a location appropriately called Compromise Landing. The Church building straddled the border between Kentucky and Tennessee, enabling the families to walk up the aisle on their side of the church and attend services, without stepping into the other state. Remarkably, half the pews were in Kentucky and half in Tennessee!

Liberty Island and Ellis Island are two small islands located in the Upper New York Bay close to Manhattan. The two islands used to be known as the Oyster Islands, named after the oyster beds that covered them and provided a source of food for the Lenape people who lived in the area before the European settlers. Liberty Island's name has changed several times. In 1667 Dutch colonist Isaac Bedloe owned the island. In 1669, colonial governor Francis Lovelace said that Bedloe could keep the ownership of the island but only if it was renamed Love Island (I have not got the imagination to make that up). Presumably, because they didn't want any "hanky-panky" taking place near New York, the name was changed to Bedloe Island in 1673 - at least they didn't change it to Fantasy Island! The Statue of Liberty was erected on the island in 1886, although it was not renamed Liberty Island until 1956. Ellis Island became known as the gateway to New York for millions of immigrants, who passed through the inspection station on the island between 1892 and 1954. It is now the centre for the Ellis Island Immigration Museum. Both Liberty Island and Ellis Island are parts of the state of New York in spite of being surrounded by waters of the state of New Jersey. How did this strange cartographic anomaly come about? In 1834, there was an interstate contract between New Jersey and New York. In 1998, the reclaimed land in New Jersey was deemed by the Supreme Court to belong to New Jersey. So, this has meant that New York has a landlocked enclave surrounded by New Jersey.

Delaware has two pieces of land that, if you study a map, look like they should be owned by New Jersey. In the 1600s, the land around New Castle, Delaware, was claimed by William Penn (see Mason-Dixon line earlier in this chapter). He was given all the land along the riverbed within a twelve-mile radius of the court building in New Castle. At the time, New Jersey's physical borders fell outside this radius. However, dredging by the US Army Corps of Engineers has expanded the landmass of New Jersey over the years. In 1934, the Supreme Court determined the low water line to be the official boundary between the states and designated the land to Delaware. This situation remains the case today, resulting in Delaware having a small enclave of land within New Jersey.

If you live in Point Roberts and have a child over ten years old, they will need to cross an international border to get to school. Point Roberts, in the state of Washington, is a tiny peninsula which is an exclave of the United States of America. It is located on the southernmost tip of the Tsawwassen peninsula near the Canadian border (south of Vancouver, British Columbia). The name of the peninsula could be included in your next spelling quiz or game of Scrabble. By the way, I spent most of my geography teaching career re-enforcing to students that Washington DC (where the White House is located) was over 4,000 kilometres (2600 miles) east of Washington state (where the Mount St. Helens volcano is located).

Unless you own a boat or seaplane, the only way to get to Point Roberts is through Canada. As a result, the town's 1,300 residents call it America's "best-gated community." Point Roberts, like so many of the Earth's most interesting places, was a geographical accident. The 1846 Treaty of Oregon drew the USA–Canada border along the 49th parallel, although no one realised at the time that this line divided the peninsula almost in half. When the mistake was discovered in London, the British pleaded with their American counterparts to let them tweak the border or work out a land swap, but the Americans refused, and Point Roberts stayed in the USA. Relations have not always been smooth between Point Roberts and its neighbours to the north. During a 1973 drought, the community's wells ran dry and Canada refused to allow access to Vancouver's water. In return, the town threatened to cut off water to Point Roberts's Canadian residents (Jennings 2012). Another place in the USA that you can't drive to without passing through Canada is, in fact, Alaska (its largest state and, as previously mentioned, the state that is its furthest north, west and east).

CHAPTER 7
ANGRY OR DISPUTED BORDERS

Travelling to the Antipodes with my wife and three young daughters in order to work in a new school was daunting enough, but not as traumatic as passing through border control to enter Australia. Not only are passports and visas scrutinised intensely, but also your luggage is examined for dairy products (not even milk is allowed for the three-year-old) and fruit. Shoes were taken off so that any soil encrusted on the sole could be inspected. Evidently, the Australians were very careful about disease entering the country (see Bumbunga micronation later in this chapter). They were paranoid about any fruit entering this continent just in case they harboured the dreaded fruit fly; there were even stricter regulations between the states within Australia. The fruit was scrumptious in this sunburnt country, especially the fresh cherries and grapes (although I much preferred the latter pressed and matured in a wine bottle). Every long and tedious car journey in Australia involved stocking up on healthy fruit snacks. It was not known to us that you could not (under ANY circumstances) carry fruit across the borders of South Australia, Queensland and New South Wales. The point where these three states meet is known as Cameron Corner, which is named in honour of John Brewer Cameron (I approve of the middle name) in the shire of Bulloo (yes, I would love to have that place on my address label). He surveyed the border in around 1880, marking the border with wooden marker posts every mile (or 1.6 kilometres). Amazingly, New Year's Eve is celebrated here three times as each of the states that meet at this corner are in different time zones. I did not realise that there are even half-hour time differences in the world, illustrated by the state South Australia which is half an hour behind the New South Wales state. The road signs made the consequences of fruit smuggling crystal clear for several miles before reaching the border. We stopped at a "driver-reviver" lay-by to eat our stock of fresh apples, oranges and cherries, not wishing to waste them in the border fruit bin or, more likely, a border guard's lunch box. By the way, at around the same time as John Cameron was marking out the state border, the pest exclusion fence (or barrier) known as the dingo fence was being built. Its purpose was to keep dingoes out of the relatively fertile south-eastern part of the continent and protect the sheep flocks of southern Queensland. It is one of the longest structures in the world, stretching 5,614 kilometres (3,488 miles) from Jimbour in the east to the north of the Great Australian Bight near Nundroo (I would love to have that name on my address as well). It protects cattle and sheep stations that are the size of small countries!

After living in Australia for a year, there is one run that I was determined to complete, with about 80,000 other runners: the "City to Surf" 14-kilometre race from Sydney city centre to the iconic Bondi beach. Upon slowly approaching the finish line and being overtaken by mostly "Love Island" look-alike contestants (and I am sure all the males were called Adonis), little did I know that I was entering an *eruv* which is a type of religious enclave. Many devout orthodox Jews believe that on the Sabbath day they are forbidden to carry anything, including a book, or umbrella, or push a pram within a public area. By stringing up a piece of wire between poles, the *eruv* is turned into a private space rather than a public one. There are *eruvin* (plural for *eruv*) in hundreds of cities around the world. It is a fence, but it doesn't exist six days out of the week.

It is a symbolic extension of the home, but not an extension of private property. It is an ingenious legal loophole to get around Jewish law that has been in existence for 1,500 years. *Eruvin* range from the size of a small front garden to over 30 square miles (such as in New York's Rockland County). In Bondi, it is constructed from a combination of the sea edge together with wires and fencing approved by the local *eruv* committee. As a result, Bondi can be regarded as a combination of a hedonistic surf and sun lifestyle with dutiful religious orthodoxy. In other parts of the world, not surprisingly, *eruvin* have caused disputes and lawsuits in the local community (Bonnett 2017). To return to the details of the fourteen-kilometre race, by the time I finished this city to Bondi run, the Sabbath was virtually over!

After studying polders in my school geography lesson, and building sandcastles on Nefyn beach in Wales to hold back the sea like King Canute, I always imagined building my own island. Up to a certain point, you can just keep depositing sand onto your island until it disappears, eroded by the waves of the powerful Irish sea. By some margin, the world's largest artificial island is an area of 970 square kilometres (375 square miles). It was built in the 1950s and 1960s in the Netherlands and is called Flevopolder. The Dutch have tried to reclaim land from the North Sea by creating dykes to keep the waters away or by draining lakes in order to produce land called polders. These polders maintain a population of about 400,000 people and are kept dry by pumping water away rather than raising the height of the dykes. If I ventured into the sea and found a new, unexplored island the name that I would call it would, I hope, be carefully considered (surely not the Cook Islands). During 1843 in the South China Sea, Richard Spratly discovered a small, low, and sandy island which he unimaginatively named "Spratly's Sandy Island". The British captain then quickly sailed off into the sunset. In 1956, a Filipino adventurer Tomas Cloma decided to "claim" a part of Spratly islands as his own, naming it the "Free Territory of...Freedomland". It looks like he wanted the island to be a free place, free of what no one is sure. As a result, a Taiwan military force was sent to occupy the largest island in the Spratly archipelago, the Itu Aba Island, as a strategic ploy. Then, in 1978, Cloma sold this entire kingdom to the Philippines for one peso (equivalent to approximately two pence), and the Philippines claimed it as their territory - a remarkable piece of business by the Philippino government!

Often called Dangerous Ground, this area of South China Sea has over forty-five contested islands, cays and reefs. As over $5.3 trillion worth of shipping travels through this area, this expanse of sea is politically sensitive (possibly this is the reason that the USA are keeping a watchful eye on this important trade route). Also, it is a marine environment that is in conflict, because the region contains 12% of the world's fish catch and an indiscernible amount of gas and oil. The five main claimants are China, Malaysia, the Philippines, Taiwan and Vietnam. It appears that the archipelago will be a flashpoint for malicious border disputes for many years to come, emphasised by one of the names of the local reefs: Mischief Reef.

If you were asked the question, which is the longest active military barrier or wall in the world, you would probably think of the Russia/China boundary or the USA/Mexico border. In fact, it is the 2,700 kilometres (1,700 miles) long Saharan Sand Wall in north-west Africa (running the equivalent length from London to St. Petersburg). It is not really a wall but a berm or raised sandbank over three metres high. Sometimes it is called the Berlin Wall of the Desert, although it is sixteen times longer than its more famous German equivalent. On the eastern side is the Sahrawi Arab Democratic Republic and on the western side is Morocco. Morocco has occupied part of its southern neighbour, Western Sahara, since 1975, when Spain, the colonial power, withdrew. The North African country fought a fifteen-year war with the Polisario Front, the independence movement of the Sahrawi Republic. Morocco decided to invade part of Western Sahara partly because of its valuable natural resources, such as phosphates and fish. Also, it is no coincidence that Western Sahara has arguably the most important fishing resources in the whole of Africa (Maclean 2018). Some Sahrawis have spent forty years as refugees in Algeria, living in temporary accommodation. They have reached middle age living in a Kafkaesque transition period without end. To make matters worse, the minefield running alongside the berm includes some of the densest landmine contamination in the world, with possibly over seven million landmines. Princess Diana tried hard to banish landmines and helped to establish the Ottawa Treaty signed in 1997 to eliminate anti-personnel mines (APs). Unfortunately, Morocco, with 31 other countries, did not sign up to the agreement. Since 2008, a demonstration against the barrier (and presumably landmines) called "The Thousand Column" is held annually in the desert by international human rights activists and Sahrawi refugees. The protest has led to a human chain demanding the demolition of the wall. Their hope remains that this berm will be worn down by the Saharan winds soon and eroded to a mere speedbump!

The Ottoman Empire (approximate dates of existence 1299-1922) ruled the whole of the Middle East at the outbreak of the First World war in 1914. It divided the region into "Vilayets", which were administrative areas based on where certain tribes lived, rather than dividing these regions into the names of countries. The Ottoman Empire was on the side of Germany and Austria-Hungary losing the First World war. Their territories were divided up following the Armistice of Mudros. Promises were made to tribal leaders regarding this land and independence when the war had finished. In 1916, a British diplomat called Colonel Sykes took a chinagraph pencil (or wax pencil) and drew a crude line across a map of the Middle East. It ran from Haifa (now in Israel) on the Mediterranean Sea to Kirkuk (now in Iraq) in the north-east. This line formed the basis of an agreement with his French counterpart, Francois Georges-Picot. It divided the region into two parts: north of the line was to be under French rule, south of the line under British control. Although the name "Sykes-Picot" line might suggest a friendship between the two men and perhaps both countries, there was a lot of mistrust between the two parties. Although there was unrest in the area even before the signing, many believe that the agreement betrayed promises to tribal leaders, which has led to continued extremism and conflict in this region. The agreement arbitrarily created examples of nation states in Africa (see chapter four, scramble for Africa) and in Arabia (see chapter five, on exclaves and enclaves) where people had never lived together before. This agreement did not lead to a peaceful outcome or any form of stability. Maps today show the borders and names of familiar countries such as Syria, Lebanon, Iraq, Israel and Jordan. Nevertheless, these countries are young and fragile nations and, unfortunately, tend to be in the Middle East's areas of conflict (Marshall 2016).

In the introduction, I briefly mentioned my high-level research on the South American country of Bolivia in a school geography lesson. Detailed investigation (highly unlikely as a fifteen-year-old) highlighted a particularly bitter border dispute between Bolivia and its neighbour Chile. The disagreement dated back to the 1879 War of the Pacific in which Bolivia lost a large portion of its territory to Chile, including its important 250 miles (400 kilometres) of coastline, and it has been landlocked ever since. It has never recovered from this land loss explaining, in part, why it is one of the poorest countries on the South American continent. This is despite Bolivia possessing the third-largest natural gas reserves in South America. Chile, on the other hand, needs a regular supply of gas. Diplomatic relations on the border have not improved as Bolivia hold out for land with their "gas for coastline policy". Another South American border dispute is shown by the British territory of Belize and its neighbour Guatemala.

The borders between these two countries are straight lines

which is not surprising because they were drawn by the British. There is a similarity between the borders mapped in the scramble for Africa (see chapter four) and the ones created when drawing the Sykes-Picot line (see above in this chapter). Guatemala claims Belize as part of its sovereign territory but, unlike Bolivia, it is unwilling, as yet, to force the issue. Paso Canoas is an international city shared between Costa Rica and Panama. The border between the two countries crosses Paso Canoas from north to south, with the result that the city is both Costa Rican and Panamanian. An important distinction is that the town is split by the border rather than being between borders. Tourists describe it as no man's land, but passport control here can be complicated with fines if your passport has not got the correct entry or exit stamp. Heavy fines have been submitted and life bans against visiting Panama if you cannot pay the fine. Perhaps not the best place to go if you have gone all that way to buy an original Panama hat because, just to add to the confusion, they are manufactured in Ecuador, not Panama (they were exported from Panama, not made there).

Chile and Argentina have argued over the Beagle Channel water route, which brought the two countries to the brink of war in 1978. The Beagle Channel (named after Charles Darwin's ship that sailed to the Galapagos Islands in 1835) lies at the tip of South America, just south of Tierra Del Fuego. An 1881 treaty between Argentina and Chile established the Beagle Channel as their international border for part of the Tierra del Fuego area, but the treaty was vague: not specifying the exact location of the channel. Of particular interest was whether the Beagle Channel border ran north of the three key islands of Lennox, Picton and Nueva (which would make them Chilean), or south of the islands (which would make them Argentinian). The issue here was not the possession of the islands themselves, which are generally cold and barren. It is that ownership of them might allow Chile to claim sovereignty or establish an exclusive economic zone 200 miles into the South Atlantic. This claim would stop Argentina's influence over islands such as the Falkland Islands (that's another story) and Antarctica (see chapter eight). Therefore, we can see that the borders in South America can be as fractious as anywhere else in the world.

Small maps on postage stamps can demonstrate border and political propaganda. On an international scale, stamps can suggest territorial claims; on a national scale, stamps can promote national unity. In Argentina, postage stamps have demonstrated claims to the Falkland Islands as well as the islands to the east held by Britain, such as South Georgia, the South Sandwich Islands and even to Antarctica. These stamps deny the legitimacy of British occupation with an "Islas Malvinas" Spanish label. Aside from South American politics, a friend told me the story of crossing the Peru to Brazil border on a coach with her boyfriend. The coach came to a standstill and, with very little use of the English language, armed border guards boarded the coach and gestured to the men to get off the vehicle. When outside, they were ordered to go to the rear and hold their hands up against the back of the coach. My friend feared the worst and could visualise desperate headlines in the newspapers back in England, never mind a distressing phone call to the parents of her boyfriend. However, it soon became clear that the only thing that the border guards wanted the men to do was to push the coach forward because it had broken down!

A micronation, by definition, is a political entity whose members claim that they belong to an independent nation or sovereign state but lack legal recognition by world governments or major international organisations. Most are geographically very small, but range in size from a single square metre to hundreds of thousands of square kilometres, for example, Westarctica (see chapter eight). Micronations have disputed borders as we have already seen in Sealand (an oil rig off the English coast see chapter six), The Republic of New Atlantis (a bamboo raft nation see chapter four), and Bir Tawil (unclaimed land between Egypt and North Sudan see chapter six). They are places offering so much promise and a chance to reinvent oneself. Liberland is a tiny parcel of land (in fact, only seven square kilometres), although we have seen that the Vatican and Monaco are even smaller. In Liberland, taxes are optional and there is no military. It is situated on the banks of the Danube between Serbia and Croatia in an unclaimed no man's land, or terra nullius territory, meaning that neither country has ever held full sovereignty over the area. Basically, it is part of a floodplain of the river, and there is no infrastructure. Vit Jedlicka, a member of the Conservative Party of Free Citizens, is the self-appointed president of Liberland. A statement announcing the creation of Liberland in 2015 read: "The objective of the founders of the new state is to build a country where honest people can prosper without being oppressed by governments making their lives unpleasant through the burden of unnecessary restrictions and taxes." The micronation has created its own currency called merits and has ambassadors in forty countries. Its motto reads: "To live and let live", which I hope is not a misquote from a James Bond film. Fifty thousand people have applied online for Liberland citizenship, but I hope they have read the fine print on the application form because, amongst others, you must not be a communist or a Nazi and not have a criminal record. To date, there has been no diplomatic recognition of Liberland by any member of the United Nations, although Sealand and Bir Tawil look like the favourites to recognise it first! Bitnation announced a partnership with Liberland in 2017. According to the internet, Bitnation is "the world's first Decentralised Borderless Voluntary Nation". Its stated purpose is to "free humankind from the oppression and sanction of pooled sovereignty, geographical apartheid and the xenophobia and violence that is nurtured by the Nation state oligopoly". It sounds like a great idea but I, for one, will not be investing any bitcoins in this micronation.

Another border dispute on the river Danube is the island of Vukovar. The peace agreement in 1992, after the break-up of Yugoslavia, decided that Croatia would control the western part and Serbia the eastern part of the Danube. Croatians were not allowed to go onto the island until 2006, when they could visit without passports or border permits. This border regime applied during the summer months, but only between 7am and 8pm to protect the island, which is a little disappointing if you want to party and drink rakija until the early hours of the morning.

Another micronation is called Ladonia, which may be one that is difficult to find because it is only one square kilometre in size and because there are no signposts or maps marking its location. It is in the Kullaberg nature reserve in north-west Skane, Sweden. In 1980, artist Lars Vilks began construction of two sculptures, Nimis (in Latin it means 'too much') - a structure made of seventy-five tonnes of driftwood - and Arx (the Latin translates as 'fortress') - a structure made of stone. The exact location of the sculptures was very inaccessible and, consequently, they were not discovered for two years. However, when they were finally located, the local council declared the sculptures to be buildings. The construction of these buildings was forbidden on the nature reserve, so the council demanded that they should be dismantled and removed. In 1996, in protest against the council, Vilks declared the micronation of Ladonia. The country has continued to have a hilariously colourful history; all chronicled on its official website (www.ladonia.org). Its chancellor, the same Lars Vilks, continued to get into trouble with the law, and in 2003, the micronation declared war on Sweden, the United States (although the *casus belli* was not entirely clear) and poor San Marino (shame, pick on someone your own size!). It has its own currency and own time zone (Ladonia Standard Time is just three minutes behind Sweden). It also has its own Ladonian Calendar, which includes holidays, such as its Independence Day, as well as more whimsical observances such as the Day of Procrastination (I need to think about observing this one), the Day of Artful Jumps, the Day of Throwing Things at Each Other and my favourite, of course, Naked Day (Ashraf 2017)! A micronation that was founded on a joke and re-elects its president using a clapometer sounds like my type of place to live in. The republic of Saugeais was founded in 1947 after a joke between the Prefect (a representative) of Doubs, a region of eastern France, and a restaurant owner who was to become Saugeais's first president. The owner of the restaurant enjoyed teasing people, so he asked the Prefect if he had a pass to enter Saugeais. The Prefect asked him to explain what Saugeais was and then said, "It looks like a Republic, but a Republic needs a President, so I declare you the President of the Republic of Saugeais". The republic has a national anthem. A banknote was released in 1997 and the French Postal Service issued a postal stamp commemorating the republic in 1987. When the restaurant owner died in 1968, the current president, his wife, was elected by the amount of applause at a party of the republic's citizens. This reminds me of the old television programme called Opportunity Knocks that judged new talent on the loudness of the clap (some people may say this is more accurate than the judges' decisions on today's television talent shows). As Churchill said, "Democracy is the worst form of government, except for all the others". This is a micronation that should not to be taken too seriously and is 'just for fun' as Hughie Green would say, referring to his clapometer, on the original television talent show *Opportunity Knocks*!

There is one micronation that you can still visit and marvel at the sight of its state border, festooned with barbed wire and designer signage. Edwin Lipburger was an Austrian artist obsessed with balls and spheres. His philosophical inspiration was: "The Earth, life, the ball, everything turns…why not live in balls?" One presumes he was not talking about Balltown in Iowa, because in 1971, Lipburger set about designing a spherical house with a diameter of over seven metres, which he called Sphaera 2000. It was built at Kugelmugel (literally, it means 'Ball Hill'), which obviously begs the question, why would you build a round house on the side of a hill? As with Ladonia (earlier in this chapter), he was ordered to demolish it by the authorities, because the sphere contravened local planning regulations. As a response, in 1976, Lipburger declared the house an independent republic, elected himself president, and began to issue his own stamps and passports, a common theme with micronations. When he refused to demolish it,

Lipburger spent ten weeks in jail and was only released after receiving a pardon from his Austrian counterpart (even though the president of the Austrian Republic has about 9 million more people to look after). The government in Austria then seized the Kugelmugel spherical house and transferred it to the Wiener Prater amusement park in Vienna. Therefore, the Republic of Kugelmugel sits there today as a tourist attraction and, in the height of irony, it is next to an enormous round Ferris wheel!

The Kingdom of Elleore occupies an island in Roskilde Fjord, in Denmark, measuring only 15,000 square metres (18,000 square yards). The island was purchased by a group of Copenhagen schoolteachers in 1944 for use as a summer camp. Their territory is actually a bird sanctuary, but environmental authorities gave the citizens permission to camp on the island for just one week per year in the month of August. This week is known as the "Elleuge" (meaning Elle-week). A justified title for a quirky island because not only is it twelve minutes behind mainland Danish time (I fail to understand why it could not be rounded up to fifteen minutes!), but the book *Robinson Crusoe* is banned. Perhaps it would have been more sensible to ban the book only on a Friday (the famous character from this Daniel Defoe's 1719 novel)!

Remaining in the European continent, the lonely island of Tavolara rises wildly from the sea like a jagged mountain located off the north east coast of Sardinia, Italy. The island is a limestone massif with one restaurant and a king who reigns over what possibly is the smallest inhabited kingdom in the world, measuring only five square kilometres. The descendants of Tonino Bertoleoni claimed the island in the nineteenth century. Queen Victoria collected photographs of leaders from around the world. She commissioned a British naval vessel to stop by the island so that officers could photograph Tavolara's "royal family". For years, the gold-framed photo was displayed in Buckingham Palace with the caption "World's Smallest Kingdom". Today, a giant copy of it hangs in Tonino's restaurant, which is appropriately called The King of Tavolara. After 126 years, the installation of a NATO base in 1962 ended the kingdom's independence and made a quarter of the island off-limits to its handful of residents. Yet, like San Marino (see chapter five), Tavolara has never been formally annexed into modern Italy. So, the king of Tavolara lords over this tiny island's eleven part-time residents, its restaurant and, of course, a hundred mountain goats (Stein 2016).

Even if you check on a map, the nearest international border to Carson City, Nevada, should be about 250 miles (400 kilometres) to the north in Canada and about 550 miles (885 kilometres) south to Mexico. However, technically there is a republic that has set up only a few miles down the road. In Dayton Valley, there is a self-proclaimed micronation called the Republic of Molossia. What would be in a guide to setting up a micronation? In order to start, you may need to choose a simple name for the country, which is not confusing. Molossia comes from the Hawaiian for harmony, *maluhia*, although it could also be confused with the ancient Greek nation of the same name. Choosing a leader, something like a king or queen, inside the USA's heartland may be better than the one Molossia decided to choose: a military dictator! It is probably best not to have too many ambitious projects if you only have thirty-three citizens - but Molossia not only has a rocket programme but a navy as well! It's a good idea to have a strong defence system - Molossia's defence capability is a dog (Fletcher 2018). However, on a positive note, this country does have its own customs office, currency and postal service. Kevin Baugh, the name of the president or dictator (or both), has a good sense of humour - the currency called the valora is tied to something valuable, not gold or the US dollar, but chocolate-chip cookie dough. The country also follows its own set of custom rules, so if you do visit, make sure that you check your luggage carefully because walruses and onions are classed as contraband goods!

Staying on the same continent of North America, North Dumpling Island is the northernmost of two islands in Fishers Island Sound, located about 550 metres north of South Dumpling Island. The two-acre (8,000 square metres) island is privately owned by Dean Kamen, inventor of the Segway Human Transporter and founder of FIRST (an organisation set up to inspire students in technology and engineering). After Kamen was denied permission to build a wind turbine on the island, he joked that he was seceding from the United States. Kamen's secession became a reality even if it is not legally recognised, but he still refers to the island as the "Kingdom of North Dumpling", and the people of North Dumpling are called "Dumplonians". He has established a constitution, designed a flag, issued the island's own currency known as the dumpling, developed a national anthem which is the sound of a stone being thrown into water and set up a navy consisting of a single amphibious vehicle. In addition to North Dumpling Lighthouse, the island has a replica of Stonehenge, hopefully the stones are lined up with the movements of the sun. The island is still part of the United States, but Kamen was able to leverage his personal relationship with the then-president George H.W. Bush to sign an unofficial non-aggression pact. Kamen, who calls himself Lord Dumpling, clearly has a sense of humour as he named the founders of Ben and Jerry's as his "Ministers of Ice Cream". Of course, the official vehicle of Dean Kamen's island nation is, as you would expect, a Segway Human Transporter!

Some micronations may be tongue-in-cheek entities, but some arise from real border disputes. In 1982, the United States Border Patrol set up a roadblock and inspection point on one of the two roads connecting the Florida Keys with the mainland. Vehicles were stopped and searched for narcotics and illegal immigrants. The local Florida council thought that the US federal government had set up the equivalent of a border station as though they were a foreign nation. So, they decided that they might as well become one. As many of the local citizens were referred to as Conchs (a slang term for people of European descent from the Bahamas), the nation took the name of the Conch Republic. As part of the protest, the mayor was proclaimed Prime Minister of the Republic, which immediately declared war against the United States of America (symbolically breaking a loaf of stale Cuban bread over the head of a man dressed in a naval uniform), quickly surrendered after one minute (to this man in the uniform), and applied for one billion dollars of foreign aid. Originally, it may have been fun, but the Conch Republic officials were invited to the Summit of the Americas in Miami in 1994, and Conch representatives were officially invited to Florida's Jubilee in 1995. The events surrounding the border blockade and the republic's independence generated great publicity for the difficulties that the Florida Keys faced. The evidence of a positive result was demonstrated by the removal of the roadblock, an increase in tourism and the comedian Billy Connolly moved into the area in 2016!

Many people believe that there are so many microstates in Australia because it was founded originally as a convict society which may have led to a general mistrust of authority. Australia has been a hotbed of micronationalism since the Principality of Hutt River was set up near Perth in 1970 after a dispute over wheat quotas. The Hutt River region lies in rolling terrain just thirty kilometres inland from the Indian Ocean in Western Australia. Fields of snow-white and sky-blue lupins, grown as high protein food for livestock, stretch towards the horizon. Leonard Casley and his wife, Shirley, and their seven children are alone in a kingdom of their own making. After many attempts to reverse a strict new quota on their production of wheat, Casley had taken the ultimate decision to split from Australia. He had many disagreements with the government resulting in the postal service refusing to handle outgoing Hutt River mail, forcing it to be diverted, remarkably, via Canada! He declared war on Australia but ceased hostilities in a week. Leonard and Shirley were deemed to be non-residents of Australia, which had the positive effect that they did not have to pay tax. A reproduction of 'Prince' Leonard's tax return is proudly mounted on the wall of the local Nain post office (Middleton 2015), presumably which is where he picks up his mail. Some Australian residents believe that Hutt River was the beginning of a long, rebellious tradition that has continued to flourish within Australia.

In 1993 the Delprat family, who lived in the suburb of Mosman in Sydney, applied to build a driveway to their house over an unbuilt road, leading to a long-running battle with the Mosman Council. It was a dispute that the family eventually lost. After threatening to build a drawbridge across his drive in 2004, Paul Delprat claimed to secede from Mosman, although not from Australia, claiming that he was a prince of the Principality of Wy (near a suburb of Sydney called Willoughby). Why Wy you may ask? Prince Paul gives this eccentric answer "Why, Willoughby begins with a W, Wy begins with a W, it's all quite wonderful my dear!" That probably says it all (Burke 2017).

Australia has over thirty micronations which probably makes it the country with the highest micronations per head of population in the world. All the leaders of Australian micronations met on Dangar Island, north of Sydney, in 2010 at their first conference. I have not been able to establish if there was any rebellious or eccentric behaviour at their meeting, although there were many characters present, some of which are outlined below.

George Cruickshank, also known as His Imperial Majesty George II of the Empire of Atlantium, set up a micro-state at Narwee, a southern suburb of Sydney. He believes that Atlantium's government is a model of future world administration. Its existence is founded on the idea that there should be global governance in a world in which there are no borders and people can live and travel freely. An interesting idea, but like any country, it needs its own parliament and monuments. Taking pride of place outside the Atlantium government building is a four-metre high pyramid, the home to this country's constitution. Emperor George II boasted this was the only pyramid in Australia; for this small country of Atlantium, with less than 3,000 residents, that is some boast (Mercer 2010)! The inhabitants drew up a constitution in 1981 decreeing a new calendar which begins at the end of the last Ice Age (at least a 10,000-year calendar). Latin became one of its official languages because "today it is a tongue that has little association with any living culture". Unlike most other countries, it advocates unrestricted international freedom of movement, so there are no passports issued. Citizens of Atlantium are true citizens of the whole world (Middleton 2015).

My favourite name of all Australia's micronations has got to be the Province of Bumbunga (I accept that the name of The Republic of Whangamomona, established in 1989, comes a close second!) Bumbunga was formed in 1976 on a rural property near the also wonderfully named Snowtown, in South Australia (nowhere near the Snowy Mountains in New South Wales). It was created by an eccentric British monarchist, Alec Brackstone, who was also a British monkey trainer and uranium prospector. He was the founder and only ruler of Bumbunga. To ensure that at least a portion of the Australian continent would always remain loyal to the British Crown, he made himself governor general. Brackstone then set about attracting tourism by planting thousands of strawberry plants in the pattern of a huge scale model of Great Britain, including its counties. Under great expense and strict supervision, soil was imported from the UK to grow the crop. He kept a separate patch on the property for patriotic expatriate British-born couples to tie the knot and claim they were married on British soil! As we saw at the start of this chapter, Australian customs authorities hate soil entering the country, even small amounts on trainers. As a result, Brackstone had to stop his enterprising weddings and eventually, the strawberries died out during a drought. In 1980, Bumbunga began issuing Cinderella stamps (believe it or not, there is a Cinderella stamp club collecting curious stamps from all over the world), portraying members of the British royal family except Sarah Ferguson, whom Brackstone disliked (I wonder which member of the royal family would not have a stamp today?) In 1999, Brackstone was arrested and charged with possession of illegal firearms. He argued that he was Bumbunga's sovereign, so that he could claim diplomatic immunity. Unsurprisingly, he lost the case (I always said that the British living in Australia is always a dangerous combination)!

The king of Tonga held an unenviable record in the Guinness Book of Records as the world's heaviest sovereign. A jovial man who was the benign ruler of a country, known since the days of Captain Cook as the Friendly Islands. However, his genial character changed in 1972 when he heard that two submerged reefs had been built up with concrete and coral blocks into small islands. They had been set up by a libertarian society who named this reclaimed artificial island in the South Pacific Ocean as the Republic of Minerva, after the Roman goddess of wisdom. As these reefs were used as Tongan fishing grounds, the gargantuan king of Tonga set off to reclaim his territory on a former English ferryboat, presumably fitted with large stabilisers. His Majesty filled the boat with dignitaries who were wearing tree-bark mats worn around the waist, a platoon of soldiers in full battledress uniform and the police brass band. Two days later, at both South and North Minerva, lifeboats were launched while the king remained aboard. Unfortunately, the final stretch before the island was too shallow, forcing the resplendent royal entourage to wade ashore across the coral. The Minervan flag was removed, hymns sung, and prayers said. A royal proclamation was read as police and military stood, still dripping wet, to attention. The landfill project that had briefly become a republic was no more as the Tongan red and white ensign was slowly raised (Middleton 2015).

There are many other micronations with disputed borders but with different stories to tell. Lizbekistan is an imaginary nation with no physical territory that had its own currency, the nipple, although I am not sure how it was represented on the back of their banknotes – perhaps they show a bust of their reigning monarch! The Kingdom of Lovely is a partly internet-based micronation created in 2006. The first-ever micronation motor race was held here, sweetly named the Lovely Grand Prix using, would you believe it, Scalextric cars! There is the Republic of Rose Island which is an artificial island constructed in 1968 by Italian architect Giorgio Rosa in the Adriatic Sea. The structure was built as a tourist attraction, but soon after it was finished, Rosa declared sovereignty. The Italian government did not like his attitude, so the navy dynamited the structure the following year! Operation Atlantis, an early 1970s

New York-based libertarian group, built a ship with a concrete hull called "Freedom", which they sailed to the Caribbean, intending to permanently anchor it as their free territory. Unfortunately, the ship sank in a hurricane and the project, as with many other plans by micronations, was abandoned!

CHAPTER 8
LIFE WITHOUT BORDERS IN THE FUTURE

In 1869 William Harvey (not the one who discovered the circulation of blood but his namesake) produced an atlas for children that he called "Geographical Fun". Many non-geographers may find this title mildly amusing, if not unattainable.

His intention was to produce an educational atlas that summed up the character of each European nation. Some may say this is what is referred to as stereotyping, which geographers today rightly spend a lot of energy trying to avoid.

Each map in his book created a caricature of what William Harvey regarded as a typical inhabitant of a country.

In order to emphasise the stereotype, each map is accompanied by a four-line poem or verse. There are a number of representations worth considering (with apologies): France has a hook-nosed empress of cooks; Spain's maiden has a bunch of grapes; Italy is a bearded revolutionary; Russia has a bear standing on its back legs. Closer to home: Scotland has a ginger and gallant bagpiper with bare hairy knees below his kilt; Ireland has a female peasant clutching a fish with a baby strapped to her back; Wales has Owain Glyndwr with a golden crown and a cloak showing a flying dragon. England is predictable for the late nineteenth century as Queen (or should we say Empress) Victoria sits in the guise of a helmeted Britannia wielding a sceptre and holding a shield of the Union Flag. This type of cartography may cause offence (hopefully not in this context), although it is meant to be "geographical fun" (Clark 2016). The purpose of these caricatures is to show that maps can be important sources of information, although not necessarily always accurate or informative. The clearly defined borders of countries, represented by the inhabitants with typical characteristics of that country, is not always a useful way to get a message across.

Zomia is the geographic term for an area in the Southeast Asian highlands, although its exact borders are controversial. The name is derived from *zomi*, a term for "Highlander" in several languages, spoken in Bangladesh, Burma, and India. James Scott (Scott 2009) identifies Zomia as "the largest remaining region of the world whose peoples have not yet been fully incorporated into nation-states". Although the precise boundaries are not certain, Scott includes all the lands at altitudes above 300 metres, stretching from the Central Highlands of Vietnam to north-eastern India. That land encompasses parts of Vietnam, Cambodia, Laos, Thailand, and Myanmar (Burma), as well as four provinces of China. Zomia's 100 million residents are minority peoples "of truly bewildering ethnic and linguistic variety," he writes. Among them are the Akha, Hmong, Karen, Lahu, Mien, and Wa peoples. Most people who ended up in the hills were either escaping the state or driven out by it. Over the past two millennia, "runaway" communities have put the "friction of terrain" between themselves and the people who remained in the lowlands. The highland groups adopted a system of subsistence agriculture (sometimes known as "slash and burn"), staggering their harvest times and relying on root crops to hide their yields from any visiting tax collectors. They form egalitarian societies so as not to have leaders who might "sell them out" to the state. Also, they turn their backs on literacy to avoid creating records that central governments could use to carry out onerous policies like taxation, conscription, and forced labour (Scott 2009).

Not that anyone would try to avoid taxes or customs tariffs on borders in Europe! So, will there be a need for more or fewer customs houses in Europe in the future? In the EU, since the Schengen agreement, some customs posts have been restored as memorials. One, on the Belgium / France border, has been converted into a chocolate shop. The old custom house between Lauterbourg in France and Berg in Germany has been converted into a restaurant and museum. There is an old customs hut between Scheibenhard in France and Scheibenhardt in Germany that is now used as a tourist information office. A paradox arises as residents rejoice due to the removal of border guards and customs officials at border stations; this contrasts with people who are concerned about many of the border buildings tending to be empty, with broken windows, peeling paint and covered in graffiti.

Setting up your own country with a government, currency and constitution with borders may seem like an April Fools' Day joke. That is what exactly happened on 1st April 1997 as the republic of Užupis was declared. Literally, it means 'beyond the river' in the Lithuanian language and it is separated from the rest of the capital city, Vilnius, by the Vilnele River. On this day in April, travellers can get their passports stamped as they cross the bridge into the republic (all other days, the border is not guarded), use the local (unofficial) currency and treat themselves to the beer that flows from the water spout in the main square. It has its own flag revealing what is known as the 'Holy Hand': a blue hand with a hole in the middle, showing they have nothing to hide in their hands (in other words, no bribes or corruption). Residents say that if you stare into the eyes of the Užupis Mermaid, a bronze bare-chested statue, as you cross the bridge into the tiny, self-declared Republic of Užupis, you'll never want to leave. Why would you want to leave if there is beer flowing from a spout? With all this going on, why is this place not on Trip Advisor's annual list of exciting places to visit? This one square kilometre republic has not been recognised officially, although the Lithuanian parliament is working on it!

The World Wide Web has become invaluable when researching

countries and locations such as Vilnius; perhaps it has become so popular that we may not realise its origins. It started in a place straddling the border between Switzerland and France. The World Wide Web was started in 1989 by Tim Berners-Lee, who was working on developing computing machinery for the European Council for Nuclear Research (in French Conseil Européen pour la Recherche Nucléaire). This is better known by the acronym CERN. Many activities at CERN now involve operating the Large Hadron Collider (LHC) and the experiments associated with it. The LHC represents a major large-scale, worldwide scientific cooperation project. The LHC tunnel is located 100 metres underground, in the region between Geneva International Airport and the nearby Jura mountains. Most of its length is on the French side of the border. The smaller accelerators are on the main Meyrin site (also known as the West Area), which was originally built in Switzerland alongside the French border. The town in France where CERN is partially situated is called Saint-Genus-Poilly. The French side is under Swiss jurisdiction and there is no obvious border within the site, apart from a line of marker stones. The repercussions of this tunnel and its research centre bestriding two European countries may lead to future revelations. Who knows, the development of the World Wide Web may appear to be insignificant compared to what CERN discovers.

There is one continent hardly discussed so far in this book that could prove to be the most vital. This continent is the windiest (an average speed of 320kmh or 198 mph), the driest (the location Dry Valleys has not seen rain for nearly two million years) and the coldest (coldest recorded temperature on earth occurred in 1983, measuring a chilly −89.2 °C). You would think it must be such an inhospitable place, yet Antarctica still attracts explorers from many different countries. This continent has no indigenous population and no permanent human population. The first woman to arrive in Antarctica was not until 1935; the first child was not born there until 1979, although I assume the two facts are not linked. The geographic South Pole is located near the Amundsen-Scott station and here, whichever way you look, you are pointing north. The South Pole is the only "undecapoint" in the world as eleven borderlines meet in one single point. These borderlines are the only *dry* borderlines which, in relation to buildings and infrastructure on the map, are constantly changing because the South Pole ice sheet is moving all the time, at the incredible rate of about nine metres per year. The UK, France, Australia, New Zealand, Norway, Argentina and Chile all recognise one another's claims on Antarctica, and their claims do not overlap. In Chile, it is illegal to publish a map that does not include Chilean Antarctica territory. Fifty-three member states have signed the Antarctic Treaty (originally signed in 1961), which says, in its article 4: "The treaty does not recognise, nor establish territorial sovereignty claims; no new claims shall be asserted while the treaty is in force." The treaty has been a success story because it has set aside the potential for conflict over sovereignty for a continent that has not required borders. Indeed, one part, Marie Byrd Land, and some islands near the coast are not claimed by any country (the only other location like this is Bir Tawil in Africa, see chapter six). Through this agreement, representatives of these countries meet every year to discuss issues as diverse as scientific cooperation, measures to protect the environment and operational issues. They have pledged to take decisions by consensus and have all made the commitment that Antarctica should not become a scene of international conflict. It begs the question, if it can be done in one continent, why cannot it be done in the remaining six continents? Unfortunately, the future may be less certain for Antarctica than the rest of the world. Its ice caps continue to melt and affect the world's sea levels. If this continues, in the future, Antarctica's protected status for science and the environment, as well as its lack of borders, may well be under threat.

The formation of micronations (for more examples, see chapter seven) may cause a threat to Antarctica. Westarctica, officially the Grand Duchy of Westarctica, is a micronation founded in 2001 by Travis McHenry. It claims the territory known as Marie Byrd Land (not claimed by any country see above), located between the New Zealand Antarctic Territory and the Chilean one, including a staggering 620,000 square miles of land, claiming over 2,000 citizens, none of which reside within the claimed territory (no surprise there!). The territory was able to be set up because of a legal loophole in the Antarctic Treaty.

So apart from the formation of Westarctica, Antarctica has somehow avoided the process of being carved up into national territories. It signposts one possible version of the future for certain parts of the world. The Antarctic transcends the norms of the Nation state, an ice-bound challenge to the global standard for territorial control. Currently, the entire continent is used exclusively for peaceful purposes, the preserve of scientists and tourists - hopefully, they are eco-tourists. This is all thanks to the Antarctic Treaty, which has become a unique agreement to govern a truly unique place (Middleton 2015).

Realistically, borders are here to stay, although not necessarily in a physical form. As we have seen (in chapter one), a bricks and mortar wall between the United States and Mexico presents a variety of logistical, environmental and operational challenges. Many of these issues could be solved through the implementation of digital border security technology, in other words, a "smart wall." Using "internet-of-things technologies" such as in-ground sensors, security cameras and software solutions, a smart wall could empower border officials to prevent illicit activity. The advantages are a quicker and cheaper implementation as well as an improvement for the natural habitat. Lower maintenance costs and no limitations on terrain are major positive factors. However, there may be issues with civil liberties, such as personal privacy. Reaper drones or UAVs (unmanned aerial vehicles to give them their proper name) can cover large border areas, up to four square kilometres, reducing the need for a physical barrier. Of course, drones can be used to send illegal goods such as methamphetamine across Mexico's border with the USA. However, there have been many examples of drones crashing because they have been overloaded with drugs. Some believe drones have an unblinking stare which many individuals call the "Gorgon Stare" named after the terrifying females of Greek mythology, the best known being the snake-headed Medusa. I understand that no drone has the technology to turn you to stone with their gaze...as yet!

CONCLUSION

When Paul Theroux was asked about why he was so interested in border crossings, he gave an enlightening insight into why these boundaries are so engaging: "The border is drama, misery, real-life, strangeness, and the actual sight of the dotted line one sees on a map. But it is usually the farthest distance from the capital, and so highly revealing of what a place is like." In order to know how a country works, Paul Theroux would always cross the border into a country rather than landing at the international airport in the capital (Shapiro 2004). In many ways, entering a country through its land borders makes sense if you want to get to know a country. Hopefully, this book has revealed some of the lighter and quirkier sides of those borders, as well as many of the sad and serious issues.

We take for granted a passport as a travel document, usually issued by a country's government to its citizens, that certifies the identity and nationality of its holder primarily for the purpose of international travel. There are serious implications for crossing borders if a passport is lost, out of date or even less than six months to the expiry date. Passports are an invaluable document dating back to Biblical times when individuals could be granted safe-conduct letters requesting that the governors of foreign lands grant them safe passage. Surprisingly, the first mention of a passport is in the Bible's book of Nehemiah from approximately 450 BC. Nehemiah, who was an official serving the king of Persia, Artaxerxes, asked permission to travel to Judea. The king granted permission for him to travel and gave him a letter requesting safe passage.

When discussing a modern passport, author Lemony Snicket sums up the absurdity of this little book:

> A passport, as I am sure you know, is a document that one shows to government officials whenever one reaches a border between countries, so the officials can learn who you are, where you were born, and how you look when photographed unflatteringly .

(JOLY 2010)

The walls and barriers discussed in this book have told their own distinct story, sometimes sad, often frustrating and at other times amusing. It is apparent from researching barriers that they have largely failed at their primary objective, which is to stop or control the movement of people and goods. Smugglers carried toilet paper through the walls in Morocco and lifted cattle over the fences in north east India. Migrant workers were led past the USA/Mexico Wall by "coyotes" (guides), and drugs were pushed through the gaps in the fence. At Halloween, children walked around L'Acadie Wall in Montreal to find sweets in previously forbidden houses. Shoppers moved across the buffer zone in the capital of Cyprus, Nicosia, in order to obtain forbidden goods and because the prices were lower. The berm in Western Sahara held valuable real estate behind it. Tourists visit The Wall on the West Bank to observe the graffiti art from now-famous artists. Black cab taxi drivers take tourists to pose for photographs against Belfast's now peaceful barriers. The scant remains of the Berlin Wall illustrate the resilience of men and women against all the odds. There is even a 'disease' created by the division caused by a barrier or wall. This syndrome is given the name "Mauerkrankheit", or wall disease (wall in the head), as discussed in chapter one. I have tried to explain that although there was anguish, horrific consequences and the break-up of families near these borders, sometimes there was hope and humour.

Generally, borders still make me nervous as a result of being stared at, searched and delayed, all with a rapid-fire gun close at hand. Some borders are simple lines, whereas others are sophisticated and technological obstacles. I have discussed whether it is worth all the effort at a frontier boundary just to cross a few metres over a bureaucratic line. Many travellers look forward to a world without borders because barriers are often seen as hostile acts of exclusion. Other tourists regard new sovereign places as an exciting prospect to explore. Baarle-Hertog thrives as a tourist destination simply because of its quirky border; Lunda Tchokwe (see chapter six) and Gaugazia (see chapter five) strive to be new nations; Sealand searches for autonomy; enclaves and exclaves suffer from excess bordering such as the Chitmahals. The paradox of borders is that they suggest a world of choices and possibility, and yet, often they can close down free movement (Bonnett 2014).

Perhaps, Baarle-Hertog is different from other border destinations. Many border issues are negated here because Belgium and the Netherlands are both in the European Union, which allows the free movement of people. It may become a different story and possibly one of chaos if either of them decides to leave the EU. However, the situation in Baarle-Hertog is a positive scenario with tourism increasing and there are many joint cross-border initiatives. The situation here is incomparable, though, to many other border regions, such as the squabbles on the Mexico/USA frontier and disagreements near the zone separating Israel and Palestine.

The future of border areas is difficult to predict: for example, who would have forecast the United Kingdom leaving an organisation that does not require border control (Brexit)? A few years ago, it would have been inconceivable to consider a 2,000-mile (3,220 kilometre) wall across south-western USA. The European Union's internal borders have been removed but its outer borders are fortified. Anyone travelling to Europe from outside the EU today comes across not only physical barriers but also the increasing use of technology. Travellers are subject to high-tech solutions (see chapter eight), such as iris eye scans, in the hope that the desire for safety can be combined with a freedom of movement once inside the EU. Without a doubt, the Schengen area has a difficult job to control a land border of approximately 8,000 kilometres (4,970 miles) and a sea border 43,000 kilometres (26,720 miles) in length. The Schengen area has nearly 600 airports to monitor, with a staggering 250 million passengers per year passing through its borders over land, 70 million people from the sea and about 390 million travellers through the air (Dijstelbloem 2011).

Some people believe that a world without borders could be a reality, arguing that the world has never been "smaller" than it is today. Digital technology can make connections in real-time across thousands of miles, allowing us to shop, work and interact internationally. Countries, businesses, organisations and people are more interconnected and interdependent than ever before. At the same time, we can travel more widely and cheaply than any previous generation and prosperity growing in many developing countries is opening up the same possibilities to millions more. The advantages for many people are undeniable as they see more growth, more innovation and possibly a more fulfilled life. However, there are serious issues linked to fewer borders on the earth. Mass migration is at unprecedented levels, often with refugee crises; terrorists and traffickers can exploit new technology and breach physical frontiers; viruses like Covid19 and diseases like Ebola are no respecters of border controls.

Many people believe that the border in the island of Ireland is the most problematic issue in Britain's turbulent departure from the European Union in 2020. The 500-kilometre (310 mile) line cuts through rivers, lakes, farms, roads and villages and separates two countries, Ireland and Northern Ireland, which have different currencies, heads of state and political systems. It also marks a division that has weighed on British and Irish history for a century, a reminder of terrorist gun-running, illicit alcohol, military checkpoints and bombs. The 208 public road crossings existing on the border is staggering. To put this into context, there are only 137 land crossings on the entire 3,720-mile frontier that separates the EU from Belarus, Moldova, Russia and Ukraine. Only a fraction of the Irish crossings were open during the conflict between the north and south in the 1970s (see chapter two). As illustrated in chapter one, some roads cross the border multiple times, while others are split along the centre. The solution may well be a futuristic technological one, perhaps based on the Swedish Customs arrangements with Norway. The proposed 'Smart Border 2.0' is based on ideas including the use of trusted trader schemes, number plate recognition cameras, customs clearance away from the border, and data sharing. The smart border arrangement has also been suggested for the Ireland and UK border.

The effects of global warming caused by climate change could be devastating to the world. Water wars could be the main reason why conflicts between countries arise in the future. As an example, Ethiopia is sometimes called "Africa's water tower" because of its high mountain elevation and over twenty dams that are fed by its high rainfall. There is a massive hydroelectric project on the Blue Nile in Ethiopia (on the Sudanese border) called the Renaissance Dam. China has invested in this dam, similarly to other projects that we have seen across the world (see chapter five). Egypt's Nile water flow, hopefully, should not be affected, but in the future, Ethiopia could hold water back, creating possible drought leading to the threat of military conflict in north east Africa (Marshall 2006).

In 2017 the island of Barbuda was hit by a category five hurricane called Irma and forced the relocation of more than 1,600 of its residents, demonstrating that climate-induced migration is no longer a future possibility, but a present-day reality. A week and a half later, Hurricane Maria knocked out power for Puerto Rico's 3.4

million residents and left much of the island without drinking water. Fifteen per cent of Puerto Rico's population (2021 figures) is expected to leave the Caribbean island and go to the mainland because of this natural disaster. A sea-level rise does not augur a dawn of fun holiday islets and resorts for low lying areas like New Moore Island (see chapter two). The majority of the Bay of Bengal, from Kolkata in the west to Myanmar in the east, may well be underwater if nothing is done. It is estimated by the IPCC (Intergovernmental Panel on Climate Change) that low-lying Bangladesh will lose 17% of its landmass by 2050. Although estimates vary, most scientists believe that there will be at least 200 million people displaced because of climate change by 2050.

Borders may have an important impact on the changing climate and our response to this issue. Severe storms blow across borders destroying human settlements throughout the world. Winds blow dust, air pollution, and rainfall across the borders. Sea level rise affects the countries that produce pollution and those that do not. Borders and sovereignty can affect environmental change and vice versa. Environmental pollution was historically produced during the industrial revolution, with countries in Europe and North America producing 68% of all emissions, while only accounting for about one-sixth of the world's population. So, although the Paris agreement on climate change was signed by virtually all states, all of them still determine their own contribution, monitor their own progress and face no consequences if they do not meet the goals that they set themselves! The countries that produced the majority of the emissions that cause climate change are now building walls and securing borders to prevent the movement of people who are displaced by it. In the year 2000, there were fifteen border walls around the world, but today there are almost seventy (Hjelmgaard 2018). Borders and sovereignty mean that countries can decide who has the right to move and can turn away even the most desperate people displaced by climate change. A dystopian future of walled states, violent borders and hundreds of millions of displaced environmental migrants is surely one that needs addressing. The world needs someone with an awareness of the issues, a vision to lead and inspire others in order to solve the global problems such as climate change, poverty and migration.

I have tried to write a book about the complexities of borders with a sense of humour and attempt, where possible, to look on the positive side (or on the 'bright side' as Michael Palin said in the film *Life of Brian*). I have discovered many curiosities: the history of UK borders is fascinating; the borders of India/Pakistan are maddening; the iron curtain is an ideological nightmare; the West Bank barrier is frustrating; the Cyprus green line is opportunistic; the USA/Mexico wall is a sporting venue; African borders are arbitrary; running across borders is exhausting; the Sykes-Picot line is somewhat erratic; enclaves are bizarre; the Schengen agreement is progressive; micronations are quirky and Antarctica is still full of hope. I never thought that I would get the chance to write and research a book on my favourite topic, and it has been an enlightening experience. As Nelson Mandela would say, "It always seems impossible, until it is done."

ILLUSTRATIONS

- Berlin Wall museum (publicdomainpictures.net.jpg)(© Jorge Royan)
- Reunion fence US / Mexico border (Flickr.com)
- Map to show Danelaw line (Imagining History)
- Union Chain bridge Scottish / English border (© Jon Cook)
- "Torpedoes" Berwick upon Tweed (© Jon Cook)
- Belfast Peace Wall (Wikimedia)
- Bar in Baarle-Hertog (Wikimedia)
- North and South Korea border (Wikimedia)
- Map of Europe (© JP Map Graphics Ltd; from book Prisoners of Geography by Tim Marshall)
- Congo panhandle (Wikimedia)
- Map of Africa (© JP Map Graphics Ltd; from book Prisoners of Geography by Tim Marshall)
- Map of North America (© JP Map Graphics Ltd; from book Prisoners of Geography by Tim Marshall)

REFERENCES

BOOK/WEBSITE/AUTHOR

1. Off the Map (2014) Alastair Bonnett
2. On the Map (2012) Simon Garfield
3. Beyond the Map (2017) Alastair Bonnett
4. Maphead (2011) Ken Jennings
5. Map Addict (2010) Mike Parker
6. Prisoners of Geography (2016) Tim Marshall
7. How to lie with maps (1996) Mark Monmonier
8. The map that changed the world (2001)
9. Pole to Pole (1992) Michael Palin
10. Sahara (2002) Michael Palin
11. An Atlas of countries that don't exist (2015) Nick Middleton
12. Down Under (2000) Bill Bryson
13. Borderline (2017) Valerio Vincenzo
14. Border (2017) Kapka Kassobova
15. Extreme Rambling – walking Israel's barrier for fun (2011) Mark Thomas
16. Walls (2012) Marcello Di Cintio
17. Mother Tongue (1990) Bill Bryson
18. Making of the British Landscape (2016) Nicholas Crane
19. The cyclist who went into the cold (2016) Tim Moore
20. All Points North (1998) Simon Armitage
21. Puckoon (1973) Spike Milligan
22. Road to Little Dribbling (2015) Bill Bryson
23. The Girl with Seven Names (2015) Hyeonseo Lee
24. Don't Go There (2018) Adam Fletcher
25. The Irresponsible Traveller – At the Border (Bradt) (2014) Tom Chesshyre
26. Atlas of the Unexpected (2018) Travis Elborough

27. African Brew Ha Ha (2010) Alan Whelan

28. I was a Potato Oligarch (2010) John Mole

29. Nathaniel's Nutmeg (1999) Giles Milton

30. Vanished Kingdoms (2012) Norman Davies

31. Maps that changed the world (2016) John Clark

32. The art of not being governed (2009) James C. Scott

33. Trieste and the meaning of nowhere (2001) Jan Morris

34. Life on the Mississippi (2021) (original 1883) Mark Twain

35. A sense of place (2004) Ed. Michael Shapiro

36. Squeezing the Orange (2013) Henry Blofeld

37. The unlikely voyage of Jack de Crow (2002) A.J. Mackinnon

38. Attention all Shipping: The Shipping Forecast (2004) Charlie Connelly

39. Kestrel for a Knave (1968) Barry Hines

40. Clear Waters Rising (1996) Nicholas Crane

41. At Home (2010) Bill Bryson

42. Cracking India (originally published as Ice Candy Man) (1988) Bapsi
    Sidhwa

43. The Dark Tourist (2010) Dom Joly

44. The Scramble for Africa (1990) Thomas Pakenham

45. Wikipedia: The Free Encyclopedia. Wikimedia Foundation, Inc. 22 July
    2004. Web. 10 Aug. 2004

ARTICLE/PROGRAMME/LYRICS

1. *Younger Generation of Cyprus unites…* Observer (14/4/19) Helena Smith

2. *The bloody road to the backstop* Observer (17/2/19) Andrew Anthony

3. *Belgium and Netherlands agree to swap land to simplify border.* Reuters –
   Guardian (29/11/16)

4. *The migration machine.* Dijstelbloem, Meijer, Besters (2011)

5. *North Korea.* National Geographic (July 2003)

6. *Czech deer still wary of iron curtain boundary.* Guardian

7. *Life between two nations.* Essay - Mark Brown

8. *Borderlines; in praise of borders.* Frank Jacobs (30/10/2011)

9. *Namibia's Caprivi Strip because the Germans forgot Victoria Falls.* Conde Nest Traveler. Ken Jennings (04/03/13)

10. *In a quiet corner of Italy...Trieste.* New York Times - Adam Begley

11. *Trieste: the Italian city that wants a divorce.* BBC - Tara Isabella Burton (31/10/14)

12. *Celebrating a nation that doesn't exist.* BBC - Sarah Reid (06/02/20)

13. *Germany's tiny geographic oddity.* BBC - Larry Bleiberg (23/09/19)

14. *Build a wall across the Sahara.* Guardian - Ruth Maclean (22/09/18)

15. *Welcome to the land that no country wants.* Guardian - Jack Shenker (03/03/16)

16. *"Sailing to Philadelphia"* (Straitjacket songs Ltd) Lyrics by Mark Knopfler (2000)

17. *Mason-Dixon line is showing its age.* Independent - Rupert Cornwall (14/10/12)

18. *The men who drew the Mason-Dixon line.* BBC - Phil Mawson (02/09/17)

19. *Bubbleland, where you will find no bubbles.* Conde Nest Traveler - Ken Jennings (05/08/13)

20. *Driving to Point Robert.* Conde Nest Traveler - Ken Jennings (05/10/12)

21. *What happens when left hand roads meet right hand roads.* Conde Nest Traveler - Ken Jennings (15/4/13)

22. *Wallyball.* Independent - Jess Staufenberg (22/08/15)

23. *Ladonia – country with 18,000 citizens.* The Daily Meal - Syjil Ashraf (08/09/17)

24. *Why....Wy.* Daily Telegraph - Kelly Burke (14/04/17)

25. *Delegates make it regal at summit.* The National - Phil Mercer (19/04/10)

26. *The World's smallest kingdom.* BBC Travel - Eliot Stein (08/03/16)

27. *Michael Palin in North Korea.* Channel 5 documentary (2019)

28. *Sara Pascoe - Last Woman on Earth.* BBC Two (January 2021)

29. *Ireland has 208 border crossings.* Irish Times - Brian Hutton (26/04/18)

30. *Mount Everest: why the summit can get so crowded.* BBC News - Helier Cheung (24/05/19)

31. *"Brownies & downieS".* https://www.Browniesanddowniesleeuwarden.nl/

32. Britney Spears. Blender Magazine (April 2004)

33. *Tourists flock to Australia's Chernobyl despite health risks.* Allyjfoster News.com.au (21/07/19)

34. *The Message in Arafat's Headdress.* Boston Globe - Jeff Jacoby (2009)

35. *Czech deer still avoid Iron Curtain.* www.bbc.co.uk (April 2014)

36. *El Paso-Juarez race reunites border 2 border cities.* Monica Uribe - NPR website (2015)

37. *Sealand: a peculiar 'nation' off England's coast.* www.bbc.co.uk - Mike Maceacheran (06/07/20)

38. *77 walls or fences around the world today.* USAtoday.com - Kim Hjelmgaard (2018)

———

INDEX

Index of places

Abkhazia, 101, 102
Adelie Land, 50
Adriatic, 4, 99, 150, 151
Alaska, 91, 116, 117, 133
Albania, 59
Alcoutim, 61
Aleutian Islands, 117
Andorra, 94, 104
Anin, 8
Aragon, 60
Argentina, 140, 141, 157
Armenia, 47, 48
Artsakh, 101
Aruba, 50
Atlantis, 86, 87
Atlantium, 149
Aust, 23
Australia, xiv, 46, 49, 73, 77, 87, 100, 121, 124, 134, 148, 149, 150, 157
Austria, 48, 65, 94, 116, 121,
Azerbaijan, 47
Azores, 48
Baarle-Hertog, 52, 53, 107, 115, 162
Balkans, xvi
Baltic, 4, 7, 91, 99, 110
Bangor-on-Dee, 97
Barbuda, 164

Beagle Channel, 140
Beit Horon, 10
Belarus, 110, 117, 164
Belfast, 36
Belize, 139, 140
Bengal, 41, 78, 165
Berchtesgadener, 94
Bering, 49, 116, 117
Berlin, vii, 4, 5, 6, 7, 63, 82, 83, 85, 86, 91, 111, 112, 118, 137, 161
Bermuda, 48, 50, 86
Berwick-upon-Tweed, xv, 28, 29, 30, 31, 32
Bir Tawil, 120, 141, 142, 157
Bogside, 36
Bolivia, xiv, 139
Bonaire, 50
Bondi, 135, 136
Boring (Oregon), 114
Boseckendorf, 68
Bosnia-Herzegovina, 108, 109
Bosporus, 70
Botswana, 82, 93
Brazil, 45, 141
Bretton Woods, 3
Bulgaria, 63, 64
Bulloo, 135

Bumbunga, 150
Burma, 1, 154,
Büsingen am Hochrhein, 106, 107
Cameroon, vii, 68, 93
Campione d'Italia, 106
Canada, 71, 72, 77, 88, 133, 146, 148
Canfranc, 60
Cape Finisterre, 65
Cape Verde, 45
Caprivi Strip, 84, 85, 93
Carham, 28
Carlisle, 33, 74
Carson City, 146
Cavan, 34
Ceuta, 91, 96
Chad, 83, 84, 93
Chepstow, 23
Cheshire, xi,
Chester, 21
Chile, 139, 140, 157
Chitmahals, 115, 162
Christiania, 47, 103
Cinco de Mayo, 72
Clones, 34
Coldstream, 28
Colne, 24
Conch Republic, 147, 148
Congo (DRC), 84, 112
Cooch-Behar, 2, 115
Cornwall, 26
Costa Rica , 81, 140
Croatia 47, 59, 105, 108, 109, 142
Cromarty, 97, 98
Curacao, 50
Cyprus, 12, 13, 15, 47, 70, 161, 166
Czech Republic, 65
Czechoslovakia, 65
Danelaw, 21, 22

Dangar, 149
Davos, 3
Denmark, xiii, 8, 20, 44, 47, 48, 145
Derry, 36,
Detroit, 71
Devon, 25, 26
Diomede Islands, 49, 116
Donegal, 35
Dorset, 25
Dover, xv
Dublin, 33
Dubrovnik, 59, 91, 108, 109
Dudley, 97
Dull (Scotland), 114
Dun Laoghaire, 33
Dunsop Bridge, 98
East Germany (GDR), 64, 67
Ecuador, 140
Egypt, 7, 48, 82, 120, 141
Ekok, 68
El Paso, 16, 72
Elleore, 48, 145
Equateur, 118
Erenhot, 124
Ethelfleda, xii
Ethiopia, 164
Everest, 41, 78
Falkland Islands, 50, 141
Famagusta, 13, 14
Ferghana Valley, 98
Finland, 44, 114
Flevopolder, 136
Florida, 81, 82, 147, 148
French Guiana, 50
French Polynesia, 50
Fundy, 71
Galapagos Islands, 140
Gambia, 92,

Gaugazia, 162
Gaza Strip, 91
Geevor, 26
Georgia, 47, 102, 141
Gibralter, 50, 91, 95, 96,
Glasgow, xvi
Greece, 57, 62, 63, 70, 86
Greenland, 20, 48
Gretna Green, 32, 33, 74
Guadeloupe, 50
Guadelupe Hidalgo, 15
Guadiana, 60, 61
Guatemala, 139, 140
Guildford, 33
Guinea, 42, 43
Gvozdev Islands, 116
Hadrian's Wall, 4, 27, 28
Haifa , 138
Halton, xii
Haltwhistle, 98
Hay-on-Wye, 23
Holy Island, 20
Hungary, 99, 116, 138
Hutt River, 148
Iceland, 20, 48
India, 2, 34, 36, 41, 74, 77, 78, 79, 80,
99, 108, 115, 154, 161, 166
Indonesia, 44, 45, 46, 50
Iraq, 138, 139
Israel, 7, 8, 9, 11, 12, 46, 138 139, 162
Istanbul, 63, 65, 70
Jamaica, xii, 121
Jerusalem, 11, 12
Jimbour , 135
Jordan, 7, 139
Kaliningrad, 91, 109, 110
Kapparis, 13,
Karakorum, 41

Kashmir, 2, 80, 81
Katanga Boot, 112
Kelso, 28
Khunjerab, 41
Kirkuk, 138
Kolkata, 165
Kongo, 118
Kugelmugel, 48, 144, 145
Kyrgyzstan, 40, 98, 99
Lancashire, xi, 24, 98
Landsker, 24
Latvia, 110
Lebanon, 139
Lesotho, 39, 40, 91
Libya, 69
Liechtenstein, 99
Lindisfarne, 20
Lithuania, 109, 110, 111, 117
Liverpool, 22, 33, 109
Lizbekistan, 151
Ljubjiana, 105
Llivia, 95
Lovely, 151
Lunda Tchokwe, 118, 162
Lundy, 25,
Luxembourg, 3
Maastricht, 53
Macau, 124
Madha, 102
Maelor, 96, 97
Mali, 68
Malin Head, 35
Malta, 47, 107, 108
Marathon, 70
Melilla, 91, 96
Mercia, xii, 22
Mexico, 15, 16, 19, 20, 72, 73, 93,
137, 146, 158, 161, 162, 166

Meyrin, 156

Mfum, 68

Minerva, 151

Moldova, 47, 100, 101, 164

Molossia, 146

Monaco, 40, 73, 142

Monaghan, 34

Mongolia, 99, 124

Montenegro, 59

Montreal, 111, 161

Morocco, 81, 86, 96, 137, 138, 161

Mosman, 148, 149

Mudros, 138

Mumbai (Bombay), 74

Myanmar, 124, 154, 165

N'Dongo, 118

Naco, 73

Nahwa, 102

Nain, 148

Namibia, 84, 85, 93

Narwee, 149

Nefyn, 136

Nepal, 41

Neum, 108, 109

Nevada, 41

New Moore Island, 42, 146, 165

Niagara, 71

Nicosia, 12, 14, 15, 161

Nigeria, 68, 93

Nogales, 16

North Berwick, 30

North Dumpling, 146, 147

North Korea (DPRK), 56

Northern Ireland, 33, 34, 38, 91, 98, 109, 164

Northumbria, xii, 21

Norway, xiii, 8, 44, 157, 164

Nundroo, 135

Offa, 22

Oldham, 24

Padstowe, 26

Palestine, 9, 11, 63, 162

Panama, 49, 140

Papua New Guinea, 49

Paris, xv, 60, 78, 83

Paso Canoas, 140

Persia, 70, 161

Perth, 87, 148

Peru, xiv, 141

Pheasant Island, 115, 116

Puckoon, 34, 35

Puerto Rico, 164, 165

Pyrenees, 57, 60, 104

Reunion, 18, 50

Romania, 67, 100

Rose Island, 151

Runcorn, xii, 71

Russia, 31, 47, 49, 61, 91, 99, 101, 102, 109, 110, 116, 117, 137, 153, 164

Saddleworth, 24

Sahara, 81, 137, 138, 161

Sahel, vii

Sahrawi Republic, 138

Saint-Genus-Poilly, 156

San Diego, 15, 19, 73

San Marino, 40, 143

Sani Pass, 39

Saugeais, 143, 144

Schengen, 3, 71, 163

Scotland, 27, 28, 29, 30, 32, 46, 74, 97, 123

Scunthorpe, 22

Sealand, 47, 121, 122, 141, 142, 162

Seborga, 106

Senegal, 42, 43, 92

Serbia, 47, 67, 142

Sheffield, 73, 74

Siam, 1, 2
Skipton, 22
Slovakia, 65, 66, 99, 116
Slovenia, 105
Snowtown, 150
Sokh, 99
Somaliland, vii
Somerset, 25
Sonora, 16, 73
South Georgia, 141
South Korea, 19, 54, 55, 81
South Ossetia, 47, 101, 102
South Sandwich Islands, 141
South Sudan, 3
South Talpatti, 41
Sparta, 70
Spice Islands, 44, 45, 46
Spratly islands, 137
Stettin, 4
Sudan, 3, 84, 120, 141
Suez, 48
Svilengrad, 63
Sweden, 114,
Syria, 7, 103, 139
Szczecin, 4
Tajikstan, 98, 99, 111
Tavolara, 47, 145, 146
Tayba, 8
Tehran, 75
Tierra Del Fuego, 140
Tijuana, 15, 19, 73
Tonga, 150, 151
Tornio River, 114
Transnistria, 2, 47, 91, 101
Trieste, 4, 104, 105,
Tunisia, 69
UAE, 102
Ukraine, 99, 100, 101 164

Ulster, 35, 36
Uzbekistan, 98, 99
Uzhhorod, 99
Užupis, 155
Varosha, 12, 13, 14
Vatican City, 40
Venezuela, 50
Venice, xiii, 40, 45, 104
Vigo, xiii
Vilnius, 155, 156
Vukovar, 47, 142
Wakhan Corridor, 111, 112
Wales, 22, 23, 24, 57, 97, 136, 153
Wank Mountain, 94
Wark, 28
Warrington, 33
Wesphalia, 102
West Bank, xii, 7, 8, 9, 10, 11, 12,
161, 166
Westarctica, 141, 157, 158
Western Sahara, 81, 137, 138, 161
Whangamomona, 150
Whitby, 22
Widnes, xi, xii, 71
Wrexham, 97
Wy, 149
Xinjiang, 99, 100
Yorkshire, 24, 98
Yugolsavia, xiii, xiv, 2, 92, 105, 108,
142
Zambia, 42, 82, 93, 112
Zamyn-Uud, 124
Zomia, 154

ACKNOWLEDGMENTS

Thank you to all those who freely gave their advice, encouragement and time.

Many thanks to Elizabeth Hague, Chenda Clark, Lord Boateng, Bernie Clifton and Bannister Publications.

Book Aid International is the UK's leading international book donation and library development charity. Every year we give millions of people the opportunity to read by providing brand new books to thousands of libraries, schools, universities, refugee camps, hospitals and prisons worldwide.

https://bookaid.org/donate/